SANKHYA-SARA

SANKHYA-SARA:

A TREATISE OF

SANKHYA PHILOSOPHY

VIJNANA BHIKSHU,
FITZ-EDWARD HALL

GYAN

Published by

GYAN

Gyan Publishing House
5, Ansari Road
Daryaganj, New Delhi-110002
Phone: 011-47034999, 9811692060
E-mail: books@gyanbooks.com

Distribution Network
gyanbooks.com
India, USA, Canada, UK, Australia

ISBN: 978-93-6780-078-2 (HB)

First Published, 1862

2nd Impression 2024

Printed at: Gyan Press, Delhi.

SANKHYA-SARA
Author: VIJNANA BHIKSHU, FITZ-EDWARD HALL

SÁNKHYA-SÁRA;

A TREATISE OF

SÁNKHYA PHILOSOPHY,

BY

VIJNÁNA BHIKSHU.

EDITED BY

FITZ-EDWARD HALL, D. C. L., OXON.,

MEMBER OF THE ASIATIC SOCIETIES OF BENGAL AND PARIS, OF THE ROYAL ASIATIC SOCIETY, OF THE AMERICAN ORIENTAL SOCIETY, OF THE ORIENTAL SOCIETY OF GERMANY, AND OF THE PHILOLOGICAL SOCIETY,

AND

H. M.'S INSPECTOR OF PUBLIC INSTRUCTION FOR THE CENTRAL PROVINCES.

CALCUTTA:

PRINTED BY C. B. LEWIS, BAPTIST MISSION PRESS.

1862.

PREFACE.*

Two systems of philosophy, attributed, respectively, to Kapila and to Patanjali, are designated, by the Hindus, as Sánkhya;† a term which common usage restricts, however,

---

* Together with the addition of much new matter, I here offer a substitute for my preface to the *Sánkhya-pravachana-bháshya.* My edition of that book is now out of print; and I have no intention of publishing another. Since writing the pages which introduced it, my views touching the Sánkhya have, owing to further study, undergone a very great change.

† The first system is known as *niris'wara;* the second, as *ses'wara.* The following half-couplet, to this effect, is from the *Shad-dars'ana-samuchchaya:*

साङ्ख्या निरीश्वराः केचित् केचिदीश्वरदेवताः ।

The Jainas claim to have their own Sánkhya, Mímánsá, &c. *Mackenzie Collection,* Vol. II., p. xxxvi.

As explanatory of the ensuing extracts, it should be mentioned, that Kapila has hitherto generally been considered as the author of the *Sánkhya-pravachana,* and that it has been the universal custom to render *niris'wara* by "atheistic."

"Cependant, il n'est guère supposable que Colebrooke se soit trompé en disant que Kapila nie l'idée de Dieu. Il n'a fait que reproduire les accusations directes que l'Inde elle-même a portées contre lui; et, comme ces accusations incontestables ne sont pas justifiées pleinement par les slokas de la Kârikâ, il reste que ce soient les Soûtras qui les justifient.. Dans aucun de ceux que nous avons traduits, cette déplorable doctrine ne s'est montrée positivement à découvert; mais je crois pouvoir affirmer, dès à présent, qu'elle est en effet dans quelques autres, comme l'affirment les commentateurs

to the former. Etymologically considered, *sánkhya* is imme-

---

indiens et Colebrooke." M. Barthélemy Saint-Hilaire: *Premier Mémoire sur le Sánkhya*, pp. 271, 272.

Again, of Colebrooke as entertaining the view, that Kapila is "atheistic:" "Il l'avait empruntée lui-même aux commentateurs indiens." Id., *ibid.*, p. 5.

This is scarcely exact. Colebrooke, the last of men to condescend, save unavoidably, to statements in train, does much more than "simply reproduce" the charge of "atheism" against Kapila, "borrowing it from Indian commentators." He refers, by numbers, to several of what have been taken for Kapila's own aphorisms, as being implicitly "atheistic;" and he translates one of them, I., 92, by the words "There is no proof of God's existence." *Miscellaneous Essays*, Vol. I., pp. 251, 252.

Alike in both the Sánkhyas, there is acknowledgment of a being superior to the gods. He is made up of an immaterial part, *purusha*, or "person," and of an *anta'karaṇa*, or "internal organ." His person is unintelligent; and, for his internal organ, by virtue of which he is intelligent, he is indebted to the promptuary of all matter, *prakṛiti*. Precisely such, it is taught, is the constitution of man, beasts, &c. Thus far both the Sánkhyas concur. But, according to Patanjali's, the Yoga, the being above spoken of, whom it calls Is'wara, has the attributes of omnipotence, omniscience, and eternalness; his material genesis being in the way of eternal and periodically recurrent emanation from *prakṛiti*. The *niris'wara* Sánkhya simply denies to any being,—even to its Hiraṇyagarbha,—the last of the attributes just enumerated. The reader is now prepared to decide, whether the doctrine ascribed to Kapila differs from the Yoga in such a manner as to justify the application to it of the epithet "atheistic;" and whether the Yoga, on the strength of its Is'wara, is entitled to the appellation of "theistic."

In the Sánkhyas, *purusha*, "person," and *átman*, "spirit," are synonymes. All that is not matter is spirit; and, as embodied, it is found in whatever possesses life, vegetation included. *Jíva*, "soul," is any spirit, in its aspect of incorporation. The Is'wara of the Yoga has no body, and is not a *jíva*. The Hiraṇyagarbha of the other Sánkhya has a body, and therefore is a *jíva*.

diately allied to *sankhyá;** a word bearing the acceptation of

"Person" and "soul," it will have been observed, are here used in senses of accommodation. And so one has to use, in general, the terminology of our metaphysics and theology, when applied to express Hindu conceptions.

On the subject of repudiating I's'wara, see the *Sánkhya-pravachana*, I., 92-99; III., 56, 57; V., 2—12, and 46; and VI., 64.

Even a limited inspection of Indian commentators on the Sánkhya would have evinced to M. Saint-Hilaire, that they are, mostly, as delicate as he is himself, in respect of charging Kapila with the denial of I's'wara. See a subsequent note.

* M. Saint-Hilaire, in the opening words of his analysis of the Sánkhya, confounds the paronymes *sankhyá* and *sánkhya*: "Le mot de Sânkhya, qui est devenu le nom du système de Kapila, signifie *nombre*; et, pris adjectivement, *numéral*. Il signifie encore, dans une acception assez voisine: calcul, supputation, jugement, raisonnement." *Premier Mémoire*, &c., p. 19.

Dr. Röer also says: "The term *Sánkhya* has two meanings, enumeration and investigation." *Lecture on the Sánkhya Philosophy*, p. 8.

The word *sánkhya*, as affording a variety of significations, is made the subject of a laborious pun, in the initial couplet of Bháskara Áchárya's *Bíja-gaṇita*.

Cháritrasinha Gaṇi, a Jaina, in his gloss on Haribhadra Súri's *Shaḍ-dars'ana-samuchchaya*, makes a statement, with reference to the origin of the word *sánkhya*, which, as being altogether novel, deserves to be produced. While acknowledging the connexion of Kapila with the Sánkhya, he avers, that the followers of that doctrine receive their appellation from the first doctor of their school, Sankha, or S'ankha. His words are: साङ्ख्यमिति कापिलदर्शनम्। शाङ्खादिपुरुषनिमित्तेयं सङ्ख्या। And elsewhere: साङ्ख्य इति पुरुषनिमित्तेयं सङ्ख्या। सङ्ख्य इमे साङ्ख्याः। तालव्यो वा शकारः। शङ्खनामाऽऽदिपुरुषः।

S'ankha, the lawgiver, is classed, with Kapila, as *támasa*, in the *Páshaṇḍotpatti* chapter of the *Padma-puráṇa*, latter section.

For an account of the *Shaḍ-dars'ana-samuchchaya*, I would refer the reader to my *Contribution towards an Index to the Bibliography of the Indian Philosophical Systems*. In that volume many particu-

"number," and also that of "decision."* But the time has

---

lars will be found, regarding books and authors, which appeared in my preface to the *Sánkhya-pravachana-bháshya,* but are here omitted.

* Colebrooke says: "A system of philosophy in which precision of reckoning is observed in the enumeration of its principles, is denominated *Sánkhya;* a term which has been understood to signify *numeral,* agreeably to the usual acceptation of *sankhyá,* number: and hence its analogy to the Pythagorean philosophy has been presumed. But the name may be taken to imply," &c. *Miscellaneous Essays,* Vol. I., p. 229.

Adverting to these words, M. Saint-Hilaire observes: "Colebrooke s'est laissé tromper par l'apparence et par une fausse analogie, en prononçant le nom de Pythagore à côté de celui de Kapila." *Premier Mémoire,* &c., p. 19.

Again, *ibid.*, p. 20: "Si Colebrooke a eu tort de rapprocher le nom de Pythagore de celui du philosophe indien," &c.

But Colebrooke, as, from his guarded and adversative mode of expression, is quite clear, delivers, in the preceding extract, neither his own opinions nor even opinions which, until the adduction of further evidence, he would be thought to accept. Professor Wilson—Oxford *Sánkhyakáriká,* Preface, p. xi.,—cites, it is true, the words "and hence its analogy to the Pythagorean philosophy has been presumed," and without comment as to the paternity of the surmise. It may have escaped him, that he had formerly written: "The first Indian school, the leading tenets of which are described by Mr. Colebrooke, is the *Sánkhya;* a term which has been understood to signify *numeral,* and which, therefore, perhaps suggested to Sir William Jones his comparison of it to the Pythagorean doctrine." *Quarterly Oriental Magazine,* Vol. IV., pp. 11, 12: for September, 1825.

Colebrooke alludes, without doubt, to the following passage: "On the present occasion, it will be sufficient to say, that the oldest head of a sect whose entire work is preserved, was—according to some authors,—Kapila; not [?] the divine personage, a reputed grandson [son] of Brahmá, to whom Kṛishṇa compares himself in the *Gítá,* but a sage of his name, who invented the *Sánkhya,* or *Numeral,* philosophy; which Kṛishṇa himself appears to impugn, in his conversation with Arjuna; and which, as far as I can recollect it from a few

long passed by for ascertaining, beyond doubt, what was

---

original texts, resembled, in part, the metaphysics of Pythagoras, and, in part, the theology of Zeno." Sir William Jones's Works, Vol. I., pp. 163, 164: 4to ed. of 1799.

Sir William, at an earlier date, had pushed his hypothetical analogies much further than this. "Of the Philosophical Schools it will be sufficient, here, to remark, that the first *Nyáya* seems analogous to the *Peripatetic;* the *second*, sometimes called *Vais'eshika*, to the Ionic; the two *Mímánsás*, of which the *second* is often distinguished by the name of *Vedánta*, to the *Platonic;* the first *Sánkhya*, to the *Italic;* and the second, or *Pátanjala*, to the *Stoic*, philosophy: so that Gautama [Gotama] corresponds with Aristotle; Kaṇáda, with Thales; Jaimini, with Socrates; Vyása, with Plato; Kapila, with Pythagoras; and Patanjali, with Zeno. But an accurate comparison between the *Grecian* and *Indian* Schools would require a considerable volume." *Ibid.*, Vol. I., pp. 360, 361.

Vijnána Bhikshu, in the *Sánkhya-pravachana-bháshya*, explains *sankhyá* to signify "the setting forth of spirit as distinct *from prakriti:*" सङ्ख्या सम्यग् विवेकेनाऽऽत्मकथनम्।

Raghunátha Tarkavágís'a Bhaṭṭácharya makes it one with "consideration:" पञ्चविंशतितत्त्वानां सङ्ख्या विचारः। तमधिकृत्य कृतो ग्रन्थः साङ्ख्य इति साङ्ख्यपदव्युत्पत्तिः सङ्गच्छते। *Sánkhya-tattwa-vilása.*

Deva Tírtha Swámin takes it to import "orderly enunciation:" कस्मात् साङ्ख्यमित्युच्यते। सम्यक् क्रमपूर्वकं ख्यानं कथनं यस्यां सा सङ्ख्या क्रमपूर्वा विचारणा। यत् तामधिकृत्य कृतं तस्मात् साङ्ख्यमित्युच्यते शास्त्रम्। *Sánkhya-taranga.*

According to a sacred text, adduced by S'ankara Ácharya, in his commentary on the *Vishṇu-sahasra-náman*, *sánkhya* means "knowledge of the true nature of pure spirit." We read:

महर्षिः कपिलाचार्यः कृतज्ञो मेदिनीपतिः।

महर्षिः कपिलाचार्य इति सविशेषणमेकं नाम महांश्चासावृषिश्चेति महर्षिः कृत्स्नस्य वेदस्य दर्शनात्। अन्ये तु वेदैकदेशदर्शनादृषयः। कपिलश्चासौ साङ्ख्यस्य शुद्धात्मतत्त्वविज्ञानस्याऽऽचार्यश्चेति कपिलाचार्यः। महर्षिश्चासौ कपिलाचार्यश्चेति महर्षिकपिलाचार्यः।

शुद्धात्मतत्त्वविज्ञानं साङ्ख्यमित्यभिधीयते।

इति व्यासस्मृतेः। ऋषिं प्रसूतं कपिलं महान्तमिति श्रुतेः। सिद्धानां कपिलो मुनिरिति स्मृतेश्च।

originally intended by thus denominating the aforesaid schemes of speculation.

The *Mahábhárata*, XIII., 7006, is here annotated.

I had hoped to find in the legal institutes of Vyása the line cited above. Not being there, probably it is buried in some Purána.

S'ankara's own definition is in these words: "The reflecting, that the *gunas*,—goodness, passion, and darkness,—are objects of my perception; and that I, distinct from them, am spectator of their operations, eternal, heterogeneous from the *gunas*, spirit." साङ्ख्यं नाम इमे सत्त्वरजस्तमांसि गुणा मम दृश्या अहं तेभ्योऽन्यस्तद्व्यापारसाक्षिभूतो नित्यो गुणविलक्षण आत्मेति चिन्तनम्। *Gitá-bháshya*, XIII., 12.

How to translate *guna* here, I know not. On this term, I shall by and by remark.

The *Mahábhárata*, a higher authority than any as yet brought forward, associates *sánkhya*, very significantly, with *parisankhyána*, which seems to have the sense of "exhaustive enumeration:"

साङ्ख्यज्ञानं प्रवक्ष्यामि परिसङ्ख्यानदर्शनम्।

XII., 11393.

Again:

साङ्ख्यदर्शनमेतावत् परिसङ्ख्यानदर्शनम्।
सङ्ख्याः प्रकुर्वते चैव प्रकृतिं च प्रचक्षते॥
तत्त्वानि च चतुर्विंशत् परिसङ्ख्याय तत्त्वतः।
साङ्ख्याः सह प्रकृत्या तु निस्तत्त्वः पञ्चविंशकः॥

XII., 11409-10.

Part of this extract is quoted in the *Sánkhya-pravachana-bháshya*, but worded somewhat differently.

Adwaitánanda, in his *Brahma-vidyábharana*, an expositorial work connected with the Aphorisms of the Vedánta, suggests, that the word *panchavins'ati*, adduced from the sacred writings as defining the number of the Sánkhya principles, may intend 20 × 5 instead of 20 + 5. This conceit might be abundantly disproved. See the stanza last given, and the *Mahábhárata*, XII., *passim*, but, particularly, chapters 307, 308, 309.

चतुर्विधं साङ्ख्यं तत्त्वप्रमाणप्रकारसर्वात्मता। What can be the drift of this mysterious announcement? It occurs in Prithwídhara Áchárya's *Ratna-kos'a*, near the end.

In the Upanishads, the *Bhagavad-gítá*, and other ancient Hindu books, we encounter, in combination, the doctrines which, after having been subjected to modifications that rendered them, as wholes, irreconcilable, were distinguished, at an uncertain period, into what have, for many ages, been styled the Sánkhya and the Vedánta.*

Though Kapila is held to have originated the distinctive tenets of the Sánkhya,† it is extremely questionable whether—

---

* It is, further, a great mistake to suppose, that the Sánkhya-yoga of the *Bhagavad-gítá* is a peculiar system of eclecticism, or of compromise, that had vogue contemporaneously with the Sánkhya and the Yoga as we now understand them. Quite unknown, in the twilight days of Kṛishṇa and Arjuna, were the distinctions which at present discriminate those systems. Kṛishṇa has much to say of Brahma: upon his predecessor, Kapila, in all probability the conception had not dawned. The idea, that Kapila denied Ís'wara, was, it is quite possible, merely inferred, long after his time, from the bare fact of his silence. Who can say that, when he lived, the notion of an Ís'wara had as yet been elaborated?

† In only a single text that I know of is the Sánkhya ascribed to S'iva. *Mahábhárata*, XII., 10388. At the same place, the Yoga also is said to have been originated by that divinity.

In the *Bhágavata-puráṇa*, I., 3, 11, Kapila is spoken of as having only revived the Sánkhya. From the same work, IX., 8, 14, it appears, however, to be asserted, that he created it. The ensuing couplet, from the last section of the *Padma-puráṇa*, is to the same purpose:

श्वेतद्वीपपतिः साङ्ख्यप्रवेत्ता सर्वसिद्धिराट् ।
विश्वप्रकाशितज्ञानयोगो मोहतमिस्रहा ॥

Vishṇu-vyúha-bheda-varṇana chapter.

A Hindu would harmonize these discordant statements by assuming, that they point to passages in two several stages of the world's history.

A facile and potential solvent of all difficulties as to time, space, and individuals, is the transparently indolent dogma of cyclical renovations of cosmic events. These iterations admitting of an indefinite

even if he was an author,—the *Sánkhya-pravachana,* now current under his name, can be referred to him on tenable grounds. And, if this "Six Lectures," at least as we possess it, is not of his composition, most assuredly neither is the *Tattwa-samása.** These works, it is observable, are nowhere cited

---

number of changes in particulars, anybody may, at last, be almost anybody else; and it thus becomes a very easy matter to make light, among other things, of ordinary chronological sequence.

Swapnes'wara, author of the *Kaumudí-prabhá,* acquainted as he was with the aphorisms of Panchas'ikha, attributes to him the "Sánkhya Aphorisms" also. He accounts for its bearing the title of *Kápila,* by the circumstance, that Kapila initiated the Sánkhya tradition as set forth therein. By way of illustration, he notes the notorious appropriation to Manu of the code of laws set forth by Bhṛigu. His meaning is, that Kapila only propounded the matter of the Aphorisms, of which the present shape is due to Panchas'ikha. He may, then, be supposed to lay to the account of humility the absence from Panchas'ikha's name, in the Sánkhya Aphorisms,—as the "Six Lectures" alone deserves to be called,—of the honorific title of *Ácháryа.* Against this it might be argued, that a saint so lowly would be likely to mention, at least a few times, the name of the leading rabbi of his school. Panchas'ikha, as we shall see, is spoken of in two places in the *Sánkhya-pravachana;* Kapila, not at all. Swapnes'wara, it should be added, gives what is here repeated, as nothing but rumour. His words are: पञ्चशिखः सूत्रकार आसुरिशिष्यः । कापिलमिति प्रसिद्धिस्तु सम्प्रदायप्रवृत्तेः भृगुप्रोक्तसंहितायामिव मनुसमाख्या ।

* Little as we can respect the allegations of Hindu writers on such a point as that before us, still it is curious to see what those allegations are.

The anonymous author of the *Sarvopakáriṇí* relates, as an ancient tradition, that Kapila the incarnation of Vishṇu composed the *Tattwa-samása,* and that, in aftertimes, another Kapila, a manifestation of Fire, published the larger body of Sánkhya Aphorisms, of which the "Compendium of Principles" was the rudiment. The same tradition makes the doctrines of other, unnamed, philosophical schools, besides the Sánkhya, no less than the Six Lectures, to have sprung

by S'ankara Ácharya, by Váchaspati Mis'ra, or by any other

---

from the *Tattwa-samása.* अथाऽतोऽनादिक्लेशकर्मवासनासमुद्रनिपतितानाथदीनानुद्दिधीर्षुः परमकारुणिकः स्वतःसिद्धतत्त्वज्ञानो महर्षिर्भगवान् कपिलो द्वाविंशतिसूत्राण्युपादिक्षत् सूचनात् सूत्रमिति हि व्युत्पत्तिः । तत एतैः समस्ततत्त्वानां सकलषष्टितन्त्रार्थानां सूचनं भवति । इतश्चेदं सकलसाङ्ख्यतीर्थमूलभूतं तीर्थान्तराणि चैतत्प्रपञ्चभूतान्येव । सूत्रषडध्यायी तु वैश्वानरावतारभगवत्कपिलप्रणीता । इयं तु द्वाविंशतिसूत्री तस्या अपि बीजभूता नारायणावतारमहर्षिभगवत्कपिलप्रणीतेति वृद्धाः ।

Vijnána Bhikshu says, *in his Sánkhya-pravachana-bháshya:* तत्त्वसमासाख्यसूत्रैः सहाऽस्याः षडध्याय्याः पौनरुक्त्यमिति चेन् मैवं सङ्क्षेपविस्तररूपेणोभयोरप्यपौनरुक्त्यात् । अत एवाऽस्याः षडध्याय्या योगदर्शनस्येव साङ्ख्यप्रवचनसंज्ञा युक्ता । तत्त्वसमासाख्यं हि यत् सङ्क्षिप्तं साङ्ख्यदर्शनं तस्यैव प्रकर्षेणाऽस्यां निर्वचनमिति । विशेषस्त्वयं यत् षडध्याय्यां तत्त्वसमासाख्योक्तार्थविस्तरमात्रं योगदर्शने त्वभ्युपगमवादप्रतिषिद्धस्येश्वरस्य निरूपणेन न्यूनतापरिहारोऽपीति । "If it be alleged, that the *Tattwa-samása* apborisms are simply iterated in the Six Lectures, the answer is, that it is not so : for there is no mere repetition between the two ; inasmuch as they are, respectively, concise and expanded. Hence, the appellation of *Sánkhya-pravachana* is suitable to the Six Lectures, in like manner as it is to the Institute of the Yoga. The former embraces precisely a detailed exposition of the *Tattwa-samása,* the shorter Sánkhya Institute. There is this difference, however ; that the Six Lectures only expands the subject-matter of the *Tattwa-samása ;* whereas the Institute of the Yoga avoids *their seeming* deficiency, by *expressly* recognizing I's'wara, whom both *the other works,* by concession for sake of argument, deny."

Our commentator, further on, grows more confident ; passing from the language of assumption, as it were, to that of positive assertion :

संक्षिप्तसाङ्ख्यसूत्राणामर्थस्याऽत्र प्रपञ्चनात् ।
शास्त्रं योगवदेवेदं साङ्ख्यप्रवचनाभिधम् ॥

"This Institute, equally with that of the Yoga, as being a development of the substance of the shorter Sánkhya Aphorisms, is designated *Sánkhya-pravachana, or,* '*Explication of the Sánkhya*'."

I am aware, that this couplet is susceptible of another construction ; but that here put upon it is unforced, and, besides, accords with the sense of the passage from the *Sarvopakáriṇí.* More than this, if the Sánkhya Aphorisms are called *Sánkhya-pravachana,* as being

writer of considerable antiquity, or even in the *Sarva-dars'ana-*

---

an expansion, it is reasonable to believe, that Vijnána designed to explain why the Yoga Aphorisms also are so designated.

Colebrooke, having in view a portion, if not all, of the foregoing extracts, writes as follows: "It appears, from the preface of the *Kapila-bháshya,* that a more compendious tract, in the same form of *sútras,* or aphorisms, bears the title of *Tattwa-samása,* and is ascribed to the same author, Kapila. The scholiast intimates, that both are of equal authority, and in no respect discordant; one being a summary of the greater work, or else this an amplification of the conciser one. The latter was probably the case; for there is much repetition in the *Sánkhya-pravachana.*

. . . .

"If the authority of the scholiast of Kapila may be trusted, the *Tattwa-samása* is the proper text of the *Sánkhya;* and its doctrine is more fully, but separately, set forth by the two ampler treatises entitled *Sánkhya-pravachana,* which contain a fuller exposition of what had been there succinctly delivered." *Miscellaneous Essays,* Vol. I., pp. 231, 232.

Dr. Röer,—*Journal of the Asiatic Society of Bengal,* for 1851, p. 402, note,—after citing the latter of the paragraphs given above, unaccountably adds: "But this is a misapprehension: the scholiast does only say 'they are of equal authority, one being a summary of the greater work, or else this an amplification of the conciser one.'" On the contrary, as will have been seen, the scholiast allows no such alternative, and is responsible for only the second member of it. Colebrooke, to be sure, has made out Vijnána to be self-contradictory. At the same time, the clause to which Dr. Röer excepts is almost a literal translation of the scholiast's own words.

M. Saint-Hilaire says, speaking of the Sánkhya Aphorisms: "Ce traité, quoique assez court, a été abrégé, dit-on, par Kapila, sous le titre de Tattva Samâsa, c'est-à-dire, réduction substantielle du Sânkhya. Nous ne connaissons ce dernier ouvrage que par les citations qu'en ont faites les commentateurs, et qu'a répétées Colebrooke d'après eux (*Essays,* tome I., p. 231)." *Premier Mémoire,* &c., p. 5

Whence did the writer learn, for certain, that Kapila abridged the *Sánkhya-pravachana?* Again, the phrase "reduction substantielle'

sangraha, which is dated so late as the fourteenth century; and

---

scarcely answers to *Tattwa-samása,* and only on the theory of such an abridgment. Moreover, Colebrooke would be explored in vain for a single quotation from the smaller treatise.

Vijnána plainly rests the validity of adjudging the title of *Sánkhya-pravachana* to the Six Lectures, on the ground, that it is an expansion of the *Tattwa-samása;* this being the embryo of also another collection of aphorisms called *Sánkhya-pravachana,* that belonging to the Yoga. But this derivation of the Yoga Aphorisms is unestablished, save by Vijnána's own word. It may be suspected, that his sole foundation of fact is, the common application of the term *Sánkhya* to the system called from Kapila and to that of the Yoga.

Colebrooke—*Miscellaneous Essays,* Vol. I., p. 232,—is disposed to think, that the title of *Sánkhya-pravachana,* in its application to the Sánkhya Aphorisms, is borrowed. For my part, I have little doubt, that one of the original borrowers was Vijnána Bhikshu. Except in the writings of that author, and of his followers, I have nowhere met with the employment of *Sánkhya-pravachana,* otherwise than to name the Yoga Aphorisms, but in the postscript to Aniruddha's commentary, and in that to its abridgment by Vedánti Mahádeva. But the epigraphs to Indian manuscripts are known to be, so generally, the work of copyists, that the adverse evidence of these two apparent exceptions may, very allowably, be neglected.

With regard to the meaning of the title *Sánkhya-pravachana,* M. Saint-Hilaire could not have done better than consult Vijnána, whose explanation of it he seems, however, to be unacquainted with. At p. 5 of his *Premier Mémoire,* &c., he translates those words by "Préface ou Introduction au Sânkhya." However speculative Vijnána may be in what he says of the germinal character of the *Tattwa-samása,* there is no ground to mistrust his etymological analysis of the word *pravachana,* as here used. In one place, as we have seen, he explains it by *prakarshena nirvachanam,* "detailed exposition;" and, in another, by *prapanchana,* "development," or "explication." In the *Pátanjala-bháshya-várttika,* he defines it, again as a member of *Sánkhya-pravachana,*—the proper name, according to Vyása, of the Yoga Aphorisms,—by words expressing "detailed statement:" सांख्यप्रवचन इति। सांख्याख्यस्यैव प्रकर्षेण वचनं सांख्यप्रवचनम्। Nágojí

their style, moreover, exhibits scarcely a perceptible trace of archaism. Indeed, the larger collection of sentences derived to us as, putatively, Kapila's, whatever its more general source, may be suspected of occasional obligation to the *Kárikás* of Ís'warakṛishṇa.*

Bhaṭṭa, in his *Pátanjala-sútra-vṛitti-bháshya-chchháyá-vyákhyá*, silently transcribes Vijnána's derivation: एतस्य साङ्ख्यप्रवचनत्वं तु साङ्ख्योक्तस्यैव प्रकर्षेण वचनात्।

* I., 124, of the *Sánkhya-pravachana* runs thus:

हेतुमदनित्यमव्यापि सक्रियमनेकमाश्रितं लिङ्गम्।

This, to a syllable, is the first half of the tenth *Káriká*.

I., 140, 141, 142, 143, 144, are as follows: संहतपरार्थत्वात्। त्रिगुणादिविपर्ययात्। अधिष्ठानाच्चेति। भोक्तृभावात्। कैवल्यार्थं प्रवृत्तेः। The seventeenth *Káriká* is read:

सङ्घातपरार्थत्वात् त्रिगुणादिविपर्ययादधिष्ठानात्।
पुरुषोऽस्ति भोक्तृभावात् कैवल्यार्थं प्रवृत्तेश्च॥

There is nothing to choose between संहत and सङ्घात, "what is combined" and "combination." Aniruddha has प्रवृत्तेः. Vijnána exchanges it for प्रवृत्तेश्च.

II., 18, further, is half a couplet:

सात्त्विकमेकादशकं प्रवर्तते वैकृतादहङ्कारात्।

The twenty-fifth *Káriká* differs only in exhibiting सात्त्विक एकादशकः; the sense remaining unaffected.

II., 31, once more, is metrical, and is the same as the last half of the twenty-ninth *Káriká*:

सामान्यकरणवृत्तिः प्राणाद्या वायवः पञ्च।

III., 48, 49, 50, 47, are as follows: ऊर्ध्वं सत्त्वविशाला। तमोविशाला मूलतः। मध्ये रजोविशाला। आब्रह्मस्तम्बपर्यन्तं तत्कृते सृष्टिराविवेकात्। And the fifty-fourth *Káriká* is

ऊर्ध्वं सत्त्वविशालस्तमोविशालश्च मूलतः सर्गः।
मध्ये रजोविशालो ब्रह्मादिस्तम्बपर्यन्तः॥

Snatches of verse, and now and then whole verses, checquer, independently of design, the prose of Sanskrit writers, as of writers in most languages. But it should be borne in mind, that the *Sánkhya-pravachana* is of very limited compass, and that the *áryá* is a measure of no little complexity. Should it be argued, with respect to the

By the prevailing suffrage of mythology, Kapila* of the

---

immetricalness of the tenth *Káriká*, that I's'warakṛishṇa there consented to a prosodial blemish, rather than deviate from the very words of an aphorism, one may answer, that, in several places where we can trace nothing like intimate dependence, on his part, upon the aphorisms which have come down to us, he is chargeable with the same sort of laxity. Instances may be seen in the fourth, seventh, ninth, twenty-sixth, and seventieth of the *Kárikás*.

Of the genuineness of the three final *Kárikás* I have grave doubt. From the seventy-second we gather nothing more than that the treatise attributed to I's'warakṛishṇa summarizes, with some reservations, the substance of the sixty Sánkhya fundamentals. It seems not altogether unlikely, that I's'warakṛishṇa may have digested into stanzas the material parts of an earlier set of Sánkhya aphorisms; that those aphorisms were long neglected, and parts of them got lost; and that the person who integrated the remnants, to make up the *Sánkhya-pravachana*, availed himself of I's'warakṛishṇa's performance.

* Professor Wilson, reviewing Colebrooke, once wrote as follows: "The founder of the *Sánkhya* philosophy is named Kapila; who, as one of the seven great Ṛishis, is one of the sons of Brahmá. There are other accounts of his origin; but none more satisfactory." *Quarterly Oriental Magazine*, for Sept., 1825; p. 12. That Kapila is any where styled "one of the seven great Ṛishis" needs confirmation, for all the emphasis with which other accounts of him are thus discredited. Nothing of this is to be found in the *Translation of the Vishṇu-puráṇa*. Colebrooke—*Miscellaneous Essays*, Vol. I., p. 229, refers, mistakingly, to Gauḍapáda, in proof of Kapila's being ranked as "one of the seven great Ṛishis." The citation runs thus:

एते ब्रह्मणः पुत्राः सप्त प्रोक्ता महर्षयः ।

"These seven sons of Brahmá were called great Ṛishis."

The more ordinary *mánasa*, or mind-born, sons of Brahmá vary, as specified in different Puráṇas, from seven to more than twice that number; "but," as Professor Wilson remarks, "the variations are of the nature of additions made to an apparently original enumeration of but seven, whose names generally recur." *Translation of the Vishṇu-puráṇa*, p. 48, note 2. One such group is made up of Maríchi, Atri, Angiras, Pulastya, Pulaha, Kratu and Vasishṭha: the

Sánkhya is held to have been a son of the god Brahmá:

---

well-known "seven Ṛishis." *Mahábhárata*, XII., 7570 and 13075. This list is modified, in the same book of the *Mahábhárata*, 7534-5; by the substitution of Daksha for Vasishṭha; and, at 13040, by the addition of Manu: the tale being thus increased to eight. But, however amplified by Pauráṇika liberality, it is not this catalogue of Brahmá's mind-born progeny that is to furnish us with Kapila.

Incidentally, the *manas*, or mind, is not located, in Hindu opinion, in the brain, as Mr. J. C. Thomson imagines. See his *Bhagavad-gítá*, p. 68, notes 4 and 7. It is thought to be in the *hṛidaya*, or breast;—not heart, as *hṛidaya* is commonly rendered.

Another company of kindred emanation likewise comprehends seven individuals. In the *Mahábhárata*, XII., 13078-9, they are said to be Sana, Sanatsujáta, Sanaka, Sanandana, Sanatkumára, Kapila, and Sanátana. In the passage quoted, in all probability from some Puráṇa, near the commencement of Gauḍapáda's commentary on the *Sánkhya-káriká*, Kapila still appears, but as introducing several accredited Sánkhya doctors, to the extrusion of as many of his former associates; the roll now standing thus: Sanaka, Sananda, Sanátana, Ásuri, Kapila, Voḍhu, and Panchas'ikha. In the *tarpaṇa*, or satisfaction-service, of at least one school of the Veda, that of Mádhyandina, the same persons are invoked, and in the same order, except that the name of Ásuri and Kapila are transposed. See Colebrooke's *Miscellaneous Essays*, Vol. I., p. 144. In the *Padma-puráṇa*, latter section, *Vishṇu-vyúha-bheda-varṇana* chapter, 14, 15, among other changes, Kapila himself makes way for another; the set now consisting of Sanaka, Sananda, Sanátana, Sanatkumára, Játa, Voḍhu, and Panchas'ikha. See the *Asiatic Researches*, Vol. XI., p. 99. The *Kúrma-puráṇa*, prior section, VII., 18, 19, with additional alterations, reduces the seven to five: Sanaka, Sanátana, Sanandana, Rúrú, (?) and Sanatkumára; whom it characterizes as great Yogins. The first three and the last of these five hold, apparently, peculiar eminence in the family of Brahmá; since from them, according to Gauḍapáda on the forty-third *Káriká*, originated, severally, virtue, knowledge, dispassion, and irresistible will. The names of these four occur, also, unaccompanied, as if they were to be regarded as representative, at III., 12, 3, of the *Bhágavata-puráṇa*.

but he is likewise described, on several occasions, as an

Sananda and Sanandana are, doubtless, prosodial varieties of the same name; and Játa seems to be put, by metrical licence, for Sanatsujáta.

In the *Kúrma-puráṇa*, latter section, V., 18, parts of the two classes of Brahmá's mental sons, several new members being added to the first, are named together, thus: Sanatkumára, Sanaka, Bhṛigu, Sanátana, Sanandana, Rudra, Angiras, Vámadeva, S'ukra, Atri, Kapila, and Maríchi. But it is worthy of observation, that this Puráṇa plainly distinguishes the second class, as to origin, from the first. What is evidently intended for the first class is detailed, at VII., 35—39, of the former section, as made up of Daksha, Maríchi, Angiras, Bhṛigu, Atri, Dharma, Sankalpa, Pulastya, Pulaha, Kratu, and Vasishṭha; and the generation of these persons, as there given, is very different from what it is in any of the accounts rendered by Professor Wilson. See *Translation of the Vishṇu-puráṇa*, p. 50, note. For instance, the first and the last four are derived, respectively, from Brahmá's *práṇa*, *udána*, *vyána*, *apána*, and *samána*. See, for these terms, Colebrooke's *Miscellaneous Essays*, Vol. I., pp. 356 and 374; also the Oxford *Sánkhya-káriká*, p. 103. At X., 84, of the *Kúrma-puráṇa*, latter section, the whole eleven are denominated Bráhmas; and Brahmá is stated to have created them by his power as a Yogin. See, also, *Translation of the Vishṇu-puráṇa*, p. 49.

Further particulars of interest occur at X., 122—125, of the latter section of the *Kúrma-puráṇa*. Sanatkumára is there said to have instructed Samvarta; and he, Satyavrata: Sanandana, Pulaha; and he, Gautama: Angiras, Bharadwája: Kapila, Jaigíshavya and Panchas'ikha: Sanaka, Parás'ara; and he, Válmíki. This Puráṇa is stated, at its conclusion, to have been transmitted from Brahmá as follows: Brahmá communicated it to Sanaka and Sanatkumára; Sanaka, to Devala; Devala, to Panchas'ikha; and Sanatkumára, to Vyása.

There is, clearly, no countenance, in the analogy of the Hindu hagiogony, for the else plausible surmise, that a complete history of the *mánasa* sons of Brahmá might, if recoverable, possibly go to show, that the epithet by which they are known may originally have borne a less mysterious signification than that of mind-born. Its intention

incorporation of Vishṇu.* Another account makes him to have been a son of Kardama;† still another gives him Dharma

---

could never have been to discriminate the literate portion of the Brahmanidae from their less learned kinsmen.

As the mind, in the Puráṇas, is constituted of matter, mental offspring are not to be looked upon as ethereal. Such, at least, is the Hindu conclusion.

* *Mahábhárata*, III., 1896 and 8880. *Rámáyaṇa*, I., 41, 2—4 and 25. At I., 41, 2—4, Kapila's destruction of the sons of Sagara is predicted. *Padma-puráṇa*, latter section, *Vishṇu-vyúha-bheda-varṇana* chapter. *Translation of the Vishṇu-puráṇa*, p. 377. *Bhágavata-puráṇa*, I., 3, 11; where Kapila stands fifth of the twenty-four incarnations of Vishṇu. See, also, at p. 5 *supra*, the verse from the *Mahábhárata*, XIII., 7006, with S'ankara Ácharya's commentary. See, further, in a coming note on Ásuri, a passage from Vyása's *Pátanjala-bháshya*. The commentators on that work, as Váchaspati Mis'ra, Vijnána Bhikshu, and Nágojí Bhaṭṭa, understand the word *ádi-vidwán*, or "primeval sage," to mean, there, Vishṇu.

Schlegel, in his note on the *Rámáyaṇa*, I., 41, 3, remarks: "De hoc Vishnûs cognomine et munere non habeo quod expromam. Vix opus est monere plane hinc alienum est *Kapilum*, philosophiae rationalis *(sánkhya)* auctorem; quamvis et hunc discipuli nimis ambitiosi numinis plenum, imo ipsum in mortali corpore praesentem Vishṇum fuisse iactaverint. Quam opinionem innuit auctor *Bhagavad-gîtae*, LECT. X., 26."

It must now appear, that the notion which Schlegel dismisses so peremptorily, is much better fortified by old report than he apprehended.

† *Bhágavata-puráṇa*, II., 7, 3; and III., 33, 1. The birth of the sage, and of his nine sisters, is there said to have taken place in the house of Kardama, the husband of Devahúti, who is called Kapila's mother. Kapila's father, according to this account, must be Kardama; as there is no hint of anything like a miraculous conception. Kapila, as thus described, is, nevertheless, regarded, by some, as having afterwards become an incarnation of Vishṇu. Kardama, if not one of Brahmá's mind-born sons, was, at all events, a *prajápati*, or "patriarch." *Translation of the Vishṇu-puráṇa*, p. 50, note.

and Hinsá for parents;* and, again, he is identified with one

---

Elsewhere, however, it is denied, that Kapila was son of Kardama by Devahúti; another and later wife of the patriarch, of unspecified name, being held for the sage's mother. As for Devahúti, she is represented as the daughter, not of Manu Syáyambhuva,—as is ordinarily declared,—but of Tṛiṇabindu. The original of these statements is expressed in the following words:

धर्मदत्त उवाच।
जयश्च विजयश्चैव विष्णोर्द्वाःस्थौ मया श्रुतौ।
किन्तु ताभ्यां पुरा चीर्णं यस्मात् तद्रूपधारिणौ ॥ १ ॥
गणावूचतुः।
तृणबिन्दोस्तु कन्यायां देवहूत्यां पुरा द्विज।
कर्दमस्य तु द्वावेव पुत्रौ द्वौ सम्बभूवतुः ॥ २ ॥
ज्येष्ठो जयः कनिष्ठोऽभूद् विजयश्चेति नामतः।
अन्यस्यामभवत् पश्चात् कपिलो योगधर्मवित् ॥ ३ ॥

Padma-puráṇa, Pátála-khaṇḍa, 97th chapter.

In Colebrooke's *Miscellaneous Essays*, Vol. I., p. 230, Devadúti is, of course, a misprint for Devahúti. Yet Professor Lassen has adopted the former reading. *Indische Alterthumskunde*, Vol. I., p. 832.

* According to the *Vámana-puráṇa*, LVI., 69—73, Dharma and Hinsá had eight sons: Sanatkumára, Sanátana, Sanaka, Sanandana, Kapila, Voḍhu, Ásuri, and Panchas'ikha. The first four were versed in the Yoga; and the rest were proficients in the Sánkhya. The passage, as I have seen it, is evidently very corrupt. I give it without any suggestions of amendment:

धर्मस्य भार्या हिंसाख्या तस्यां पुत्रचतुष्टयम्।
सम्प्राप्तं मुनिशार्दूल योगशास्त्रविचारकम् ॥
ज्येष्ठः सनत्कुमारोऽभूद् द्वितीयश्च सनातनः।
तृतीयः सनको नाम चतुर्थश्च सनन्दनः ॥
साङ्ख्यवेत्तारमपरं कपिलं वोढुमासुरिम् ॥
दृष्ट्वा पञ्चशिखं श्रेष्ठं योगयुक्तं तपोनिधिम् ॥
तांश्च योगं न ते दद्युर्ज्यायांसोऽपि कनीयसाम्।
सान्तमुग्रं महायोगं कपिलादीनुपासतः ॥
सनत्कुमारश्चाऽभ्येत्य ब्रह्माणं कमलोद्भवम्।

of the Agnis, or Fires.* Lastly, it is affirmed, that there have been two Kapilas: the first, an embodiment of Vishṇu; the

---

अगच्छद् योगविज्ञानं तमुवाच प्रजापतिः ।
ज्ञानयोगं न ते दद्युर्ज्यायांसोऽपि कनीयसाम् ॥

The first three of these stanzas are adduced in the *S'abda-kalpa-druma*, pp. 1831—32; where they are erroneously said to be from the fiftieth chapter of the *Vámana-puráṇa*.

* प्राकाश्यागतिर्देवो यो बिभर्ति हुताशनम् ।
अकल्मषः कल्मषाणां कर्ता क्रोधाश्रितस्तु सः ॥
कपिलं परमर्षिं च यं प्राहुर्यतयः सदा ।
अग्निः स कपिलो नाम साङ्ख्ययोगप्रवर्तकः ॥

Mahábhárata, III., 14196—7.

The last line of these verses is cited by Vijnána, near the conclusion of his *Sánkhya-pravachana-bháshya*. But he rejects, with indignation, the idea, that Kapila is therein identified with Fire. It is simply meant, he says, that Kapila was endowed with the potency of fire; and he supports his interpretation by the aid of analogy, with some ingenuity. Of there having been two Kapilas, he will hear nothing.

In his version of it, the line he quotes is so phrased, as to give Kapila the authorship of the Sánkhya only, and not of the Yoga likewise:

अग्निः स कपिलो नाम साङ्ख्यशास्त्रप्रवर्तकः ।

Professor Wilson, writing of this text, of whose respectable origin he was uncertified, pronounces, touching the identity it authenticates, that "there does not appear to be any good authority for the notion," and adds, immediately afterwards: "*Kapila* is a synonyme of fire; as it is of a brown, dusky, or tawny, colour; and this may have given rise to the idea of Agni and the sage being the same." Oxford *Sánkhya-káriká*, p. 188. See, also, Colebrooke's *Miscellaneous Essays*, Vol. I., p. 230. But it seems just as likely, that the notion owed its origin to the fabled combustion, by Kapila, of the sons of Sagara. *Mahábhárata*, III., 8881. Also see the *Asiatic Researches*, Vol. III., pp. 349, 350; and Vol. VI., p. 478.

For Colonel Wilford's wild speculations, in which he makes Kapila one with Enoch, *vide ibid.*, Vol. VI., pp. 473-4.

other, the igneous principle in corporeal disguise.* It must

---

* See the reference to the *Sarvopakárini*, in the foot-note at p. 8, *supra*.

S'ankara Ácharya, in the *S'áríraka-mímánsá-bháshya*, I., 2, 1, also declares for two Kapilas. Implicitly following the *Rámáyana*, he considers the Ságaracide Kapila to be an incarnation of Vásudeva, or Vishnu; but he denies the origination, or revival, by him, of the Sánkhya philosophy. It is in another Kapila, on whom he forbears to expatiate, that he recognizes its inventor. The *Bhágavata-purána*, IX., 8, 13, insists, that this Kapila could not, with his benevolent nature, have slain the Sagaridæ intentionally. Yet it makes no doubt, that they were destroyed by fire issuing from the body of the incensed ascetic, independently of his volition.

S'ankara Ácharya, commenting on the word Kapila in the *S'wetás'watara-upanishad*, V., 2, proposes two interpretations of it. By one of them it is violently made to denote, as a lame synonyme, Hiranyagarbha. Otherwise, since primogeniture among created beings is found averred of both Kapila and Hiranyagarbha, they are, to save scriptural consistency, concluded to be one and the same. On the other interpretation, the person named in the Upanishad is Kapila of the Sánkhya, a partial incarnation of Vishnu. For his character as such, some unnamed Purána is adduced. S'ankara adds, that the other Kapila is celebrated in the *Mundaka-upanishad*. This statement is, however, made inadvertently; since no mention of him occurs there. S'ankara probably quoted, after the ordinary reckless Indian fashion, from memory. Dr. Röer has somewhat misrepresented S'ankara, in making him cite suicidally the Purána above referred to. S'ankara avowedly cites it, not to corroborate the first identification of Kapila, but to elucidate the second. Neither, in that quotation, is Kapila, "to praise him," "identified with Hiranyagarbha." See the *Bibliotheca Indica*, Vol. XV., p. 62.

It may be observed, generally, that, in conformity with Hindu usage, none but the predilective object of one's idolatry is glorified as a plenary incarnation.

Kapila, in the *Mahádeva-sahasra-náma-stotra*, *Mahábhárata*, XIII., 1211, is an epithet of S'iva, and expresses, as indicated by the context, "tawny."

be acknowledged, in sum, that we know nothing satisfactory concerning our old-world sage; the meagre notices of him that are producible being hopelessly involved in uncertainty, and inextricably embarrassed by fable. Yet it may be credited, with but little hesitation, that he was something more substantial than a myth;* and there is good ground for our receiving, as an historical fact, his alleged connexion with the Sánkhya.

In an inscription translated by Colebrooke, there occurs the word *kapilá*, which, he observes, "probably is fire, personified as a female goddess." [sic] *Miscellaneous Essays*, Vol. I., p. 300, last line; and p. 304, foot-note No. 21. It remains to be shown, that the word ever means fire. In that place it bears, undoubtedly, the sense of "dun cow;" from circumambulating which sort of creature great merit is supposed to be acquired. "'A red one:' *kapilá*. When applied to a cow, this term signifies one of the colour of lac-dye, with black tail and white hoofs." Colebrooke's *Two Treatises on the Hindu Law of Inheritance*, p. 131, second foot-note. For *kapilá*, in this acceptation, see the *Mahábhárata*, XIII., 2953, 3535, 3596, 3703-4, 3744, 3764; and, on the subject of circumambulating a cow, see the same poem, XIII., 3436 and 3794.

* Colebrooke comes to a different conclusion. "It may be questioned," he says, "whether Kapila be not altogether a mythological personage, to whom the true author of the doctrine, whoever he was, thought fit to ascribe it." *Miscellaneous Essays*, Vol. I., p. 231. But the *Mahábhárata*, despite its plentiful alloy of fiction, sufficiently attests, it should seem, the reality of the sage; and the *Sánkhya-pravachana* and *Tattwa-samása* may be pseudonymous, without vacating the existence of Kapila, or his character of Sánkhya proto-philosopher.

There is, I doubt not, much new matter about Kapila in Dr. Muir's *Sanskrit Texts*; but, to my regret, the work is not, at this moment, accessible to me.

In the *Padma-puráṇa*, latter section, *Gaurí-viváha-varṇana* sub-division of the *Kumára-sambhava* chapter, Kapila is said to have dwelt in the village of Indraprastha. Further particulars regarding this personage can, doubtless, be obtained, if the *Kapila-upapuráṇa*,

Among the ancients whose names are found in association with that of Kapila, are Ásuri, Panchas'ikha, Sanátana, and Sanandana. These five persons, with others, we have mytho-historical authority for classing as brothers. But accounts differ on the subject of their parentage. An option is allowed between regarding them as mind-born sons of Brahmá,* and as offspring, after the natural course, of Dharma and Hinsá.†

Ásuri, it is stated, had for teacher Kapila himself.‡ That he was an author, we have the evidence, such as it is, of a single couplet.§

---

which is named in the *Kúrma-puráṇa*, and elsewhere, be still extant. For the *Kapila-sanhitá*, a colloquy concerned with the sacred localities of Orissa, see Dr. Aufrecht's *Catalogus Cod. Manuscript. Sanscrit*, &c., p. 77. At p. 26 of the Sanskrit Catalogue of the library of the Asiatic Society of Bengal, occurs the name of *Kápila-smṛiti*, or Legal Institute of Kapila. A work on naval astrology, attributed to Kapila, has been found in the Peninsula. *Mackenzie Collection*, Vol. I., p. 262. A treatise on the Yoga, called *Kapila-gítá*, has also fallen in my way. It professes to be extracted from the *Padma-puráṇa*.

* See the note at p. 14, *supra*.

† See the note at p. 17, *supra*.

‡ *Bhágavata-puráṇa*, I., 3, 11. Panchas'ikha *apud* Vyása: *Pátanjala-bháshya*, I., 25: आदिविद्वान् निर्माणचित्तमधिष्ठाय कारुण्याद् भगवान् परमर्षिरासुरये जिज्ञासमानाय तन्त्रं प्रोवाच। The commentators are unanimous in understanding, by *paramarshi*, or "great Ṛishi," Kapila.

Colebrooke—*Miscellaneous Essays*, Vol. I., p. 231,—speaks of this passage as being one of Panchas'ikha's *sútras*. But it is not so discriminated by Vyása, or by Vyása's commentators; though they name Panchas'ikha as its author. Colebrooke, it is clear, did not suspect, that reference was anywhere made to more than one work of Panchas'ikha.

§ विविक्ते दृक्परिणतौ बुद्धौ भोगोऽस्य कथ्यते।
प्रतिबिम्बोदयः स्वच्छे यथा चन्द्रमसोऽम्भसि॥

This I found in Cháritrasinha Gaṇi's scholia on the *Shaḍ-dars'ana-samuchchaya*.

Panchas'ikha is called a disciple of Ásuri;* but he is also said to have been instructed by Kapila.† He is known, by scanty fragments, as an aphorist.‡ Of a second work of his we have indications,§ and, it may be, of a third. It is manifest,

---

* *Mahábhárata*, XII., 7890, 7895.

† And to have been fellow-student of Jaigíshavya. *Kúrma-puráṇa*, Prior Section, IX., 119. See, further, the reference to the *Kúrma-puráṇa* in the note at p. 15, *supra*.

If Colebrooke—*Miscellaneous Essays*, Vol. I., pp. 229, 230,—meant to intimate, that, in Gauḍapáda's commentary, Panchas'ikha is spoken of as Kapila's disciple, either directly, or through Ásuri, he committed an oversight. That Ásuri was Panchas'ikha's preceptor is declared in the seventieth *Káriká*; but on that couplet Gauḍapáda makes no remark.

‡ A single one of his aphorisms is given, as such, in Vyása's *Pátanjala-bháshya*, I., 4: **एकमेव दर्शनं ख्यातिरेव दर्शनम्।** Kshemánanda, in his notes on the *Tattwa-samása*, twice quotes this as a *sútra*; and Váchaspati Mis'ra, Vijnána Bhikshu, and Nágojí Bhaṭṭa, consent in assigning it to Panchas'ikha.

In Vyása's *Pátanjala-bháshya* we find, at II., 13: **स्वल्पः सङ्करः सपरिहारः सप्रत्यवमर्षः कुशलस्य नाऽपकर्षायाऽलम्। कस्मात् कुशलं हि मे बह्वन्यदस्ति यत्राऽयमावापगतः स्वर्गेऽप्यपकर्षमल्पं करिष्यति।** Of this passage,—which is uncharacterized, by Vyása, except as being by Panchas'ikha,—the *Sánkhya-tattwa-kaumudí* cites the words **स्वल्पः सङ्करः सपरिहारः सप्रत्यवमर्षः।** So does Náráyaṇa Tírtha, in his *Bhakti-chandriká*. Swapnes'wara, in his annotations on the *Kaumudí*, still dissecting, says, that the first three of these words form one aphorism, and the remaining word, another.

So much for Panchas'ikha's *sútras*; and it may be questioned whether any more samples of them are forthcoming, notwithstanding Colebrooke's assertion, that they "are frequently cited, and by modern authors on the *Sánkhya*." *Miscellaneous Essays*, Vol. I., p. 233.

§ This work is metrical; unless, indeed, the longer extracts, to be given after the ensuing couplets, belong, with one or more of them, to a treatise mixed of prose and verse.

that he wrote on the Sánkhya; and it is not impossible, that

आद्यस्तु मोक्षो ज्ञानेन द्वितीयो रागसंक्षयात्।
कृच्छ्रक्षयात् तृतीयस्तु व्याख्यातं मोक्षलक्षणम्॥

This couplet is quoted, by Vijnána Bhikshu, in his *Brahma-sútra-ṛiju-vyákhyá*, with the following introduction: त्रिविधं मोक्षं प्रमेयाऽन्त तत्त्वसमासाख्यभाष्ये पञ्चशिखाचार्यः। This is the best voucher we have for the opinion, that Panchas'ikha commented on the *Tattwa-samása*, of which the words त्रिविधो मोक्षः do really constitute a topic. This couplet is again quoted, partially, by Vijnána, in his *Yoga-várttika*, as well as in Bhávágaṇes'a's *Yogánus'ásana-sútra-vṛitti;* and in full, by Kshemánanda on the *Tattwa-samása*, in the *Sánkhya-krama-dípiká*, and by Bhávágaṇes'a in the *Tattwa-yáthárthya-dípana.* Its various readings, and those of the stanzas following, are not of sufficient importance to call for particularization.

Bhávágaṇes'a, in his *Yogánus'ásana-sútra-vṛitti*, refers the stanza just given, directly to Panchas'ikha; but, in his *Tattwa-yáthárthya-dípana*, he introduces those verses, and the three couplets subjoined, by expressions importing, that they were borrowed, not from, but through, Panchas'ikha.

पञ्चविंशतितत्त्वज्ञो यत्र कुत्राऽऽश्रमे स्थितः।
जटी मुण्डी शिखी वाऽपि मुच्यते नात्र संशयः॥

प्राकृतेन तु बन्धेन तथा वैकारिकेण च।
दक्षिणाभिस्तृतीयेन बद्धोऽयं तु निगद्यते॥

तत्त्वानि यो वेदयते यथावद् गुणस्वरूपाण्यधिदैवतं च।
विमुक्तपाप्मा गतदोषसङ्घो गुणांस्तु भुङ्क्ते न गुणैः स युज्यते॥

Now, these three couplets, and that preceding them, the first and the third as acknowledged quotations, are also found in the *Sánkhya-krama-dípiká*. The last two are cited both there and in the *Sánkhya-sútra-vivaraṇa*. The first has been spoken of above; and the second is in Kshemánanda on the *Tattwa-samása*, in Cháritrasinha Gaṇi on the *Shaḍ-dars'ana-samuchchaya*, and is twice given in Gauḍapáda on the *Sánkhya-káriká*. It is, besides, observable, that Bhávágaṇes'a does not quote a syllable as derived through Panchas'ikha, that does not occur in the *Sánkhya-krama-dípiká*. There is, accordingly, a presumption, that Bhávágaṇes'a took the passages from that work, and under the impression, that it was by Panchas'ikha; and

he was likewise an expounder of the dogmas of Patanjali.

---

this suspicion is strengthened by the second exordial stanza of the *Tattwa-yátharthya-dípana*, where its author clearly enough claims to have consulted Panchas'ikha on the *Tattwa-samása*:

समाससूत्रमालम्ब्य व्याख्यां पञ्चशिखस्य च।
भावागणेशः कुरुते तत्त्वयाथार्थ्यदीपनम्॥

The attribution to Panchas'ikha of the *Sánkhya-krama-dípiká*, if ever actually maintained, would at once be invalidated by indicating the fact, that mention of Panchas'ikha is made, in the work itself, supposed free from interpolation; and in such a manner, namely, with the title of *áchárya*, as to differentiate him from its author.

The passages extracted below have, in every case, the guarantee of good authority for their being by Panchas'ikha. They are given, in the first instance, by Vyása, in his *Pátanjala-bháshya*, anonymously: but three of Vyása's commentators, Váchaspati Mis'ra, in the *Pátanjala-sútra-bháshya-vyákhyá*, Vijnána Bhikshu, in the *Yóga-várttika*, and Nágojí Bhaṭṭa, in the *Pátanjala-sútra-vṛitti-bháshya-chchháyá-vyákhyá*, testify, one, or all, to their authorship. As for the passage at II., 22, Váchaspati merely says, that it is by an *ágámin*, or authoritative sage: the two other scholiasts declare it to be by Panchas'ikha.

The first of the annexed passages is quoted and elucidated by Kshemánanda, in the *Nava-yoga-kallola*. A few words from the passage at II., 20, are brought forward in the concluding chapter of the *Sarva-dars'ana-sangraha*.

तमणुमात्रमात्मानमनुविद्याऽस्मीत्येवं तावत् सम्प्रजानीत इत्येषा द्वयी विशोका-विषयवत्यस्मितामात्रा च प्रवृत्तिर्ज्योतिष्मतीत्युच्यते यया योगिनश्चित्तं स्थितिपदं लभते। I., 36.

व्यक्तमव्यक्तं वा सत्त्वमात्मत्वेनाऽभिप्रतीत्य तस्य सम्पदमनुनन्दत्यात्मसम्पदं मन्वानस्तस्य व्यापदमनुशोचत्यात्मव्यापदं मन्वानः स सर्वोऽप्रतिबुद्ध इत्येषा चतुष्पदा भवत्यविद्या मूलमस्य क्लेशसन्तानस्य कर्माशयस्य च सविपाकस्य। II., 5.

बुद्धितः परं पुरुषमाकारशीलविद्यादिभिर्विभक्तमपश्यन् कुर्यात् तत्राऽऽत्मबुद्धिं मोहेन। II. 6.

तत्संयोगहेतुविवर्जनात् स्यादयमात्यन्तिको दुःखप्रतीकारः। कस्मात्। दुःखहेतोः परिहार्यस्य प्रतीकारदर्शनात्। तद् यथा पादतलस्य भेद्यता कण्टकस्य भेत्तृत्वं परिहारः कण्टकस्य पादानधिष्ठानं पादत्राणव्यवहितेन वाऽधिष्ठानम्। एतत् त्रयं यो वेद लोके स तत्र प्रतीकारमारभमाणो भेदजं दुःखं नाऽऽप्नोति। कस्मात्। त्रित्वोपलब्धिसामर्थ्यात्। II., 17.

Sanátana is reported to have busied himself with the Yoga; but none of his writings seem to have survived to the present day.*

Sanandana, at least in the acknowledgment of tradition, was a philosopher of high repute. Of his literary remains, if he left any, nothing, it is believed, has reached us.†

Except at sheer random, we can scarcely estimate the duration that divided Ís'warakṛishṇa from Kapila. The utmost that can, with any safety, be said of his time is, that he flourished before the ninth century. In the very abruptness with which he begins his compendium,‡ the manner of a compar-

---

अयं तु खलु त्रिषु गुणेषु कर्त्तृष्वकर्त्तरि च पुरुषे तुल्यातुल्यजातीये चतुर्थे तत्क्रियासाक्षिण्युपनीयमानान् सर्वभावानुपपन्नाननुपश्यन् न दर्शनमन्यत् शङ्कते। II., 18.

अपरिणामिनी हि भोक्तृशक्तिरप्रतिसंक्रमा च परिणामिन्यर्थे प्रतिसंक्रान्तेव तद्वृत्तिमनुपतति। तस्याश्च प्राप्तचैतन्योपग्रहरूपाया बुद्धिवृत्तेरनुकारमात्रतया बुद्धिवृत्त्यविशिष्टा हि ज्ञानवृत्तिरित्याख्यायते। II., 20.

धर्मिणामनादिसंयोगाद् धर्ममात्राणामप्यनादिः संयोगः। II., 22.

रूपातिशया वृत्त्यतिशयाश्च परस्परेण विरुध्यन्ते सामान्यानि त्वतिशयैः सह प्रवर्त्तन्ते। तस्मात्संकरः। यथा रागस्यैव क्वचित् समुदाचार इति न तदानीमन्यत्राऽभावः किन्तु केवलं सामान्येन समन्वागत इत्यस्ति तदा तत्र तस्य भावस्तथा वृत्तस्य। III., 13.

तुल्यदेशश्रवणानामेकश्रुतित्वं सर्वेषां भवति। III., 40.

Little can safely be conjectured with regard to the character of the work, or works, from which these sentences were selected by Vyása. They may be text; and they may be commentary. Probably they are Sánkhya; but, possibly, they pertain to the Yoga.

* Ráyamukuṭa, in his *Pada-chandriká*, cites from the *Yoga-s'ata-kákhyána* of a Sanátana; and Sundara Deva, in his *Haṭha-sanketa-chandriká*, a Yoga treatise, from the *Sanátana-siddhánta*.

† He is one of the two authorities referred to by name in the *Sánkhya-pravachana;* where he enjoys, uniquely, the honour of being called an *áchárya*. It may be, that this notice of him is in an aphorism retained from the original *Sánkhya-sútra*.

‡ Its opening stanza is translated as follows by Colebrooke, Professor Lassen, Dr. C. J. H. Windischmann, and M. Saint-Hilaire:

atively early ago is plainly perceptible: he invokes no divinity,

---

"The inquiry is into the means of precluding the three sorts of pain: for pain is embarrassment. Nor is the inquiry superfluous, because obvious means of alleviation exist; for absolute and final relief is not thereby accomplished."

"E tergeminorum dolorum impetu (oritur) desiderium cognoscendae rationis qua ii depellantur. Quod (cognoscendi desiderium) licet in visibilibus rebus infructuose versetur, non est (infructuosum) propter absentiam absoluti et omni aevo superstitis (remedii)."

"Wegen des Zudrangs der Dreiheit von Leiden entsteht das Bestreben nach Erkenntniss eines diese (Leiden) verdrängenden (radicalen) Heilmittels. Sagt man: Dieses Bestreben sey unnüz, da ein sichtbares (Mittel der Abwehr) vorhanden sey, so ist dies falsch wegen des Nichtseyns eines vollständigen und dauernden (Mittels)."

"La philosophie consiste à guérir les trois espèces de douleurs. Si l'on prétend qu'il existe des moyens matériels de les guérir, et que, par conséquent, la philosophie est inutile, on se trompe; car il n'est pas un seul de ces moyens qui soit absolu ni définitif."

If the intended sense, in the first line, were "for pain is embarrassment," the formation of the sentence being considered, the Sanskrit should be दुःखत्रयस्याऽभिघातत्वात्. Dr. Windischmann—*Die Philosophie im Fortgang der Weltgeschichte*, pp. 1812, 1813,—concurs with Professor Lassen on the point here controverted, but afterwards copies Colebrooke almost literally. Váchaspati Mis'ra explains the beginning of the couplet to concern "the disadvantageous connexion of the intelligent power, *or soul*, with threefold pain resident in the internal organ:" दुःखत्रयेणाऽन्तःकरणवर्तिना प्रतिकूलतया चेतनाशक्तेरभिसम्बन्धोऽभिघातः। Professor Lassen's "impetus" is not at all "irreconcilable with the context," as Professor Wilson has pronounced it to be. For the rest, I quite agree with the former in preferring Váchaspati's तदपघातके to तदभिघातके. The *Káriká* will then, run thus:

दुःखत्रयाभिघाताज् जिज्ञासा तदपघातके हेतौ।
दृष्टे साऽपार्था चेन् नैकान्तात्यन्ततोऽभावात्।

I would render it: "Because of the discomposure *that comes* from threefold pain, *there arises* a desire to learn the means of doing away therewith *effectually*. If *it be objected, that,* visible *means to this end*

and salutes no venerable preceptor, but enters at once upon his

---

being available, such *desire* is needless, I demur; for that *these means do* not, entirely and for ever, *work immunity from discomposure*."

Abhighâta signifies "impact," "blow," "shock," "agitation." *Apaghâta* has the sense of "averting," "debarring," "removal," "elimination." *Drishṭa*, "visible," is for "worldly," or "physical." Colebrooke puts "obvious."

The French interpretation of the preliminary *Káriká* is hardly an inspiration of profound scholarship. Yet a critique of it may not be amiss. In the first place, the relation of identity is never, as there assumed, expressed, in Sanskrit, by the fifth case. More strangely still, in manifest ignorance of the manner in which more than one set of Hindu aphorisms commences, M. Saint-Hilaire understands *jijnásá* to denote "philosophy;" herein silently adopting Professor Lassen's inference, based on the consideration of its etymology: *Gymnosophista*, p. 18. But the mere "ambition to know" would be too vague and indeterminate, by far, for the highest aspiration of the Hindu. Philosophy, with him, is a concretion, a definite *tattwa-jijnásá*, or "desire of apprehending first principles." It may be mentioned, parenthetically, that Professor Wilson has misread Gauḍapáda, where he explains जिज्ञासा by the equivalent desiderative विविदिषा; as this does not imply "by the wise," which would be विविदुषा,—or, rather, the plural; if, in fact, such an adjective as विविद्वस्, though not abnormal, be ever used.

Another error, on the part of M. Saint-Hilaire, and equally important with the one just disposed of, consists in the anachronism of representing I's'warakṛishṇa as employing a style of phraseology which would reduce him to the last century, and even transport him to the fellowship of antichristian Parisians. With most people but Frenchmen, the contrast to revelation is reason alone. So it is with us; and the same is the case with the Bráhmans, whose word for "reason" is *yukti*, never *jijnásá*. No more than the Vedánta itself is the Sánkhya a school of naturalism. The Bauddhas, the Chárvákas, and a few other classes of Indian religionists, openly and unreservedly disown the warrant of the Veda; but, on the other hand, as Colebrooke has most justly observed, the Sánkhyas "endeavour to reconcile their

undertaking, without ceremony or circumlocution. Who he was,

---

doctrine to the text of the Indian scripture, and refer to passages which they interpret as countenancing their opinions. The *Mímánsá*, which professedly follows the *Veda* implicitly, is, therefore, applied in its controversy with these half-heretics, to the confutation of such misinterpretations. It refutes an erroneous construction, rather than a mistaken train of reasoning." Like the rest of the six great systems, the Sánkhya, it is true, imposes some share of its dogmas upon the Veda, and then claims to have extracted them from it: a course which has had its precise parallel in procedures connected with our own Holy Writ. Still, its free-handling is by no means overdone, if we judge by the Indian standard.

M. Saint-Hilaire, in the course of his remarks on the first *Káriká*, adduces the introductory sentence of those imputed to Kapila: "L'objet définitif de l'esprit de l'homme, c'est la cessation définitive de la triple douleur." On this, and the two aphorisms which succeed it, he says: "La traduction de ces trois Soûtras de Kapila nous montre fort nettement quel a été le travail de l'auteur de la Kârikâ. Il n'a rien changé à la pensée primitive, et il l'a suivie pas à pas: seulement il l'a rendue plus précise; il l'a même abrégée."**** Ainsi, dès le premier pas, la Kârikâ, comme les Soûtras, établit l'objet de la philosophie." This is very gratuitous. Where, in the first three aphorisms, do we see anything about *jijnásá*, M. Saint-Hilaire's hypothetical "philosophie"? The complete cessation of threefold pain is there enunciated to be the supreme purpose of the soul. On M. Saint-Hilaire's theory, that I's'warakṛishṇa adheres undeviatingly to the intent of the aphorist, "la philosophie," the contradistinguished from revelation, must have been substituted, by him, for "l'objet définitif de l'esprit de l'homme."

Proceeding to the second *Káriká*, we find the expression दृष्टवदानुश्रविकः, "the revealed mode is like the temporal one," as Colebrooke has it. Yet all revelation is not here contemplated. The commentators are of opinion, and rightly, that only the Vaidika ritual is animadverted upon. What is inculcated is, that a man should not restrict himself to sacrifice and like observances, the promised requital whereof is confined to the inferior bliss of Elysium, and stops short of ensuring a period to the grand evil of existence, metempsychosis, and where he dwelt, are, however, questions that must, it seems, for ever go unanswered. One writer, to be sure, styles him disciple of Panchas'ikha;* and another will have it, that he and Kálidása were the same person:† but these statements though worthy of record, would require strong confirmation before they could challenge acceptance.

Those works which the Hindus style non-voluntary,—among which sacrifice is comprehended,—are, indeed, said to be attended with sin: nevertheless, whatever the sin of performing them, there would be greater sin in abstaining from them. Being prescribed, they must be *done*; and the consequences must be endured, and duly atoned for. The Sánkhya simply takes a flight beyond the legalistic Mímánsá: and so does the Vedánta; no more than which does the Sánkhya cut itself away from the Veda, or lay a ban upon the rites and ceremonies which it is thought to enjoin. In a word, the Sánkhya would only dissuade from content with a lower grade of future happiness. M. Saint-Hilaire's phrase of "reste de respect pour l'écriture sainte," used of a Sánkhya, proceeds, then, from misapprehension; and equally so does his remark on the first two *Kárikás*: "L'autorite de la raison n'a jamais été plus nettement affirmée; sa suprématie n'a jamais été plus hautement proclamée."

* Náráyaṇa Tírtha, in the *Tattwa-chandra*, so describes him, and gives him the title of Muni.

† Swapnes'wara says, in the *Kaumudí-prabhá*: ईश्वरकृष्णनाम्ना कालिदासेन कृताः कारिकाः। These words are continuous with the extract given in a foot-note to p. 8, *supra*. The only MSS. of the *Kaumudí-prabhá* that I have seen,—two in number,—are defective at the conclusion, where Swapnes'wara may, perhaps, have enlarged on the traditional identity which he reports.

Kavirája Yati, author of the *Sánkhya-tattwa-pradípa*, calls I's'wara-kṛishṇa *sánkhya-múla-kára*, or "founder of the Sánkhya." This may have been intended as nothing more than a compliment. As such I have more than once heard the epithet applied, by the pandits, to the compiler of the *Sánkhya-káriká*.

Colebrooke, prior to the date of his elaborate and fruitful researches on Hindu philosophy, wrote as follows: "The text of the *Sánkhya*

The next writer that here calls for notice is one of foremost importance. Of all extant treatises on the system of Kapila, by much the most valuable are those of Vijnána Bhikshu. While he unfolds the doctrines of the Sánkhya with a completeness such as leaves little to be supplemented, he has the merit, in his capacity of expositor, of being as cautious as he is copious. If none of his countrymen have added to him, neither has any one of them ventured to arraign his accuracy,* still less, to disallow his ability.

---

philosophy, from which the sect of Buddha seems to have borrowed its doctrines, is not the work of Kapila himself, though vulgarly ascribed to him; but it purports to be composed by I's'warakṛishṇa." *Miscellaneous Essays*, Vol. I., p. 103. Unquestionably, this sentence was penned while Colebrooke was as yet unacquainted with the so-called aphorisms of Kapila; and it must have escaped his eye; when he was recommitting his essays to the press.

* M. Saint-Hilaire, indeed has found fault with him; but the reader shall see how misapprehensively.

First of all, I subjoin the twenty-fifth *Káriká*, with Colebrooke's translation, and the censurer's:

सात्त्विकं एकादशकः प्रवर्त्तते वैकृतादहङ्कारात्।
भूतादेस्तन्मात्रः स तामसस्तैजसादुभयम्॥

"From consciousness, affected by goodness, proceeds the good elevenfold set: from it, as a dark origin of being, come elementary particles: both issue from that principle affected by foulness."

"L'ensemble des onze principes donés de bonté émane du moi quand il est modifié également par la bonté. Du moi considéré comme élément primitif viennent les éléments grossiers; il est alors obscur; et cette double émanation n'a lieu que par l'influence de l'activité."

Now, the expression "origin of being" is, in this place, all but nugatory: and Professor Wilson's assumption, that "origin of beings" is intended, does not at all mend the matter; since "beings," in the only plausible sense of which the word is here susceptible, that of "creatures," or "elemental creation,"—fifty-third *Káriká*,—are, out of the Puráṇas, produced from egoism only by the intermediate agency of the elementary particles.

His reputation as an author rests upon at least five works,

The mistake which Professor Wilson falls into, after his attempt to correct Colebrooke, can easily enough be accounted for. Gauḍapáda says: भूतानामादिर्भूतः। तमोबहुलस्तेनोक्तः स तामस इति। This the Professor translates thus: "The first element of the elements is darkness; therefore it is usually called *the dark*." But the word here rendered by "first element" would, as masculine, mean "first being," if it were a substantive; "first element" requiring, not *ádibhútah*, but *ádibhútam*. Being, however, an adjective, it refers to *bhútádi*, the second factor of which it justifies etymologically. This reference should have been evident from the gender of *uktah*, *sa*, and *támasa;* and also from that of *bahulas*, which could never be an adverb. It is not propounded, that the elements originate from their like, from an element; and, while nothing is predicated of darkness, darkness is predicated as characterizing one of the varieties of egoism. The passage cited above will, therefore, admit of no other translation than such as this: "It, *origin of the elements*, is originant, *viz.*, of the elements: *it is* surcharged with darkness, *and* hence is called dark." To bear out Professor Wilson's English, the Sanskrit should have stood somewhat after this sort: भूतानामाद्यभूतं तमः। तेन बहुधोक्तं तत् तामसमिति।

In giving the passage from Gauḍapáda, I have supplied it with punctuation, and the only punctuation that it will abide.

In the *Vishṇu-puráṇa*, at I., 12, 53, the term *bhútádi* "generative of the elements," epithetically employed in place of "dark egoism," is again rendered, by Professor Wilson, "first element." See his Translation, p. 93, line 12.

Professor Wilson, building on his oversight, indulges in the following comment, which may now be cancelled: "There is a remarkable expression in the *Bháshya*, which presents a notion familiar to all ancient cosmogonies. Gauḍapáda says, 'the first of the elements was darkness.' It is the first of the 'elements,' not the first of 'things;' for it was preceded by unevolved nature, and intellect, and it is itself a modified form of individuality. It therefore harmonizes perfectly well with the prevailing ideas in the ancient world, of the state of things anterior to elementary or visible creation, when 'chaos was, and night,' and when

all of them concerned with philosophy. Their titles, in the

Nullus adhuc mundo praebebat lumina Titan,
Nec nova crescendo reparabat cornua Phœbe.

In the influence of the quality of foulness, or passion,—for the word *rajas* has both senses,—may be suspected an affinity to the doctrine of an active principle, the moving mind, the *eros*, that set inert matter into motion, and produced created things." Oxford *Sánkhya-káriká*, p. 94.

Professor Lassen, who was the first to translate the whole of Ís'wara-kṛishṇa's treatise; has a right understanding of *bhútádi.* "Caterva undenum essentialis proficiscitur e sui sensu essentiali; rudimentalis ex (sui sensu) elementorum generatore; haec caliginosa est. Ex impetuoso (sui sensu) utralibet oritur creatio." Twenty-fifth *Káriká*, in *Gymnosophista*, p. 58.

Professor Wilson's remarks, incidentally bearing on the functions of *bhútádi*, at p. 164 of the Oxford *Sánkhya-káriká*, are unsubstantiated. The text on which those observations are founded is as follows: एवमभौतिकः सर्गो लिङ्गसर्गो भावसर्गो भूतसर्गो दैवमानुषतैर्यग्योना इत्येष प्रधानकृतः षोडशसर्गः। "Thus, non-elemental creation, rudimental creation, conditional and elemental creation, in beings of divine, mortal, brutal, and (immovable) origin, are the sixteen sorts of creation effected by nature." Instead of this, we should certainly read: "The non-elemental creation,—*i. e.*, the rudimental creation and the conditional creation,—and the elemental creation, *or the aggregate of* beings of divine, mortal, and brutal, origin, are the sixteen sorts of creation proceeding *mediately* from nature."

My MS. wants the word भूतसर्गो "elemental creation:" but its insertion, as an equivalent of the भौतिकः सर्गः of the fifty-third *Káriká*, is quite immaterial. Moreover, I have corrected a grammatical inadvertence.

The elemental creation has fourteen divisions; and the two branches of the non-elemental count, each, as unity. The sum of sixteen is thus completed. There is, then, no such successive correlation, in the above passage, as may have led the Professor to supply the word "immovable," and which induced him to make the following comment: "Apparently, each of the four classes of beings proceeds from

order, mainly, in which they were composed, here follow.

---

four modifications of nature; or, from the invisible principles, from the subtile rudiments, from the conditions or dispositions of intellect, and from the gross elements."

The evolution of the Sánkhya principles, as recited in the *Vishṇu-puráṇa*, is strangely misrepresented by the translator. A single specimen will suffice.

भूतादिस्तु विकुर्वाणः शब्दतन्मात्रिकं ततः ॥
ससर्ज शब्दतन्मात्रादाकाशं शब्दलक्षणम् ।
शब्दमात्रं तथाऽऽकाशं भूतादिः स समावृणोत् ॥

I., 2, 37-8.

"Elementary Egotism then becoming productive, as the rudiment of sound, produced from it Ether, of which sound is the characteristic, investing it with its rudiment of sound." P. 16.

The correct rendering is: "The element-engendering *egoism*, being modified, then produced the rudiment of sound; *and*, from the rudiment of sound, the ether, of which the characteristic is sound: *and* this element-engendering *egoism*, similarly *to agents in processes before mentioned*, invested the ether, which consists of sound."

Almost the entire page from which the passage above touched on is taken, is disfigured by the style of misapprehension just pointed out. In one place, in fact, in order to force the construction desired, the nominative singular *váyú*—euphonically required for *váyuh*—is made accusative. Saintly liberties vastly more licentious than this are often taken, in the Puráṇas; but there is, in this instance, no temptation whatever to do violence to Páṇini.

To return to M. Saint-Hilaire. Part of his comment on the twenty-fifth *Káriká* is thus expressed: "Or Vidjnâna comprend qu'il s'agit ici, non pas de l'ensemble des onze principes sortant du moi, mais du onzième principe, c'est-à-dire, du manas, du cœur, qui, dans toutes les classifications, figure régulièrement, comme on l'a vu, au onzième rang, parce qu'il est tout à la fois organe de perception et organe d'action. Il faudrait donc faire ici un changement considérable, et substituer le manas aux onze organes.

* * * * * * *

"Si l'on adopte l'explication de Vidjnâna, il faudrait traduire le vingt-cinquième sloka de la façon suivante: 'Le onzième principe doué

I. The *Brahma-sútra-ṛiju-vyákhyá,* sometimes called *Vijnánám-*

---

de bonté émane du moi quand le moi est modifié également par la bonté; du onzième principe, considéré comme élément primitif, viennent les éléments grossiers. Ce onzième principe est obscur; et tous deux, ce principe et le moi, n'agissent que sous l'influence de l'activité.'

"Mais on peut remarquer que cette explication est en contradiction formelle avec les slokas qui précèdent: d'abord, avec le sloka vingt-deuxième, qui fait sortir directement du moi les seize principes, et qui fait sortir en particulier les éléments grossiers des éléments subtils; et ensuite, avec le sloka vingt-quatrième, qui reproduit la même doctrine. Il faut ajouter que cette doctrine que nous retrouvons dans la Kârikâ vient de Kapila lui-même, comme le prouve le soûtra que nous avons cité. Nous devons donc nous en fier à l'explication de Gaoudapada plutôt qu'à celle de Vidjnâna. Dans le système sânkhya bien interprété, les cinq éléments grossiers viennent des cinq éléments subtils; et les cinq éléments subtils, avec les onze organes, viennent du moi. Ce n'est pas le manas, le cœur, qui produit les éléments grossiers, comme le croit Vidjnâna Bhikshou; et ce qui doit nous étonner encore davantage dans son erreur, c'est que, dans le soûtra immédiatement précédent, Kapila dit expressément, lecture deuxième, soûtra dix-septième: 'L'effet du moi, c'est l'ensemble des onze organes et des cinq éléments grossiers.' Quelque délicat qu'il soit de se prononcer dans des questions de ce genre, nous croyons pouvoir affirmer que Vidjnâna Bhikshou s'est trompé, et qu'il n'y a point à tenir compte de son opinion." *Premier Mémoire,* &c., pp. 100—102.

The critic, misled by Professor Wilson's "first element," translates *bhútádi* by "élément primitif." He also substitutes "éléments grossiers" for éléments subtils," as an evolution from his "élément primitif;" thus passing by the origin of the subtile elements, which, themselves directly derived from egoism, constitute the immediate source of the gross elements.

In order to adjust the twenty-fifth *Káriká* after Vijnána's conception of *manas,* M. Saint-Hilaire correctly premises, that this word, denoted by "the eleventh," must be substituted, in the couplet, for "eleven." But, professing to effect this substitution, while he once puts *manas* therefor, he puts it three times for "egoism." He also puts

ṛita ; a commentary on the Vedánta Aphorisms of Bádaráyaṇa.

---

egoism for "subtile elements," or, rather, "gross elements :" for he foists this blunder of his own, as well as his borrowed "primitive element," on the injured commentator. Vijnána was not the man to perpetrate such a solecism as the deducing any of the elements from mind. He expands the text of the *Sánkhya-pravachana*, II., 17, in these words : "The eleven organs, and the five subtile elements, *to-wit*, sound, &c., are the products of egoism :" एकादशेन्द्रियाणि शब्दादिपञ्चतन्मात्रं चाऽहङ्कारस्य कार्यमित्यर्थः। How could this have escaped the critic's eye ?

But Vijnána has clearly enough set forth his view of the twenty-fifth *Káriká ;* as M. Saint-Hilaire would have seen, had he only mastered, even with the aid of Professor Wilson,—a little closely scrutinized,—the scholiast's understanding of the eighteenth Aphorism of the second Book. After alleging *manas* to mean the eleventh organ, Vijnána explains "both" to refer to the intellectual organs and the organs of action : एकादशानां पूरणमेकादशकं मनः षोडशात्मगणमध्ये सात्त्विकम्। एतच्च वैकृतात् सात्त्विकाहङ्काराज् जायत इत्यर्थः। एतस्य राजसाहङ्काराद् दशेन्द्रियाणि तामसाहङ्काराच् च तन्मात्राणीत्यवगन्तव्यम्। * * * * * उभयं ज्ञानकर्मेन्द्रिये। The *Káriká* will, then, run thus : "The eleventh *organ*, consisting of goodness, originates from modified egoism. From *egoism, as* the source of the elements, *proceed* the elementary particles ; *and* this *variety of egoism is* imbued with darkness. From *egoism* affected by activity, arise both *the intellectual organs and the organs of action*."

Vijnána is, therefore, peculiar, as compared with some others, in deriving from pure egoism but a single educt, mind, instead of eleven, viz., mind and the ten organs of intellection and action : the latter being referred, by him, to the active species of egoism ; which is held, on the adverse interpretation, to be, independently, inoperative, but yet an indispensable condition of energy on the part of the other two manifestations of the self-conscious principle. Whether *ekádas'akam*, in the aphorism, stands for "eleven," or for "eleventh," is altogether uncertain. Aniruddha takes it to be for the former. That Vijnána deals with the *Káriká* unjustifiably, in respect of *ubhayam*, is not to be gainsaid. At the same time, the Aphorisms stand uncommitted to the doctrine clearly implied thereby. We here have an addition,

II. The *Sánkhya-pravachana-bháshya*, or *Sánkhya-bháshya*; a commentary already spoken of. III. The *Pátanjala-bháshya-várttika*, or *Yoga-várttika*; annotating Vyása's commentary

---

in the *Kárikás*, which ill comports with the theory, that they were derived, by abridgement, or otherwise, from the *Sánkhya-pravachana* as we now have it.

The productiveness of active egoism is the doctrine of the Puráṇas. For instance:

भूततन्मात्रसर्गोऽयमहङ्कारात् तु तामसात्।
तैजसान्यिन्द्रियाण्याहुर्देवा वैकारिका दश॥
एकादशं मनश्चात्र देवा वैकारिकाः स्मृताः।

Vishṇu-puráṇa, I., 1, 46-7.

"This is the elemental creation, proceeding from the principle of egotism affected by the property of darkness. The organs of sense are said to be the passionate products of the same principle, affected by foulness; and the ten divinities proceed from egotism affected by the principle of goodness; as does mind, which is the eleventh." Professor Wilson's Translation, pp. 17, 18.

In a foot-note to p. 16, the Professor repeats Gauḍapáda's account of the three sorts of egoism, but without directing attention to its contradiction of his text.

For a passage to the same effect with the verses given above, see the *Bhágavata-puráṇa*, III., 5, 29 seqq.: also III., 26, 27 seqq. The first of these two passages is cited by Vijnána on II., 18, of the *Sánkhya-pravachana*. Víraràghava, in his commentary, the *Bhágavata-chandriká*, wrests the word *taijasát*, in the fourth verse, into congruity with the dogmas of I's'warakṛishṇa and his school, by explaining it to denote "with the aid of passional *egotism*."

Add: वैकारिकादहङ्कारात् सर्गो वैकारिकोऽभवत्।
तैजसानीन्द्रियाणि स्युर्देवा वैकारिका दश॥
एकादशं मनश्चात्र स्वगुणेनोभयात्मकम्।
भूततन्मात्रसर्गोऽयं भूतादेरभवन् प्रजाः॥

This is from the *Kúrma-puráṇa*, Prior Section, IV. It will be found, probably quoted from memory, in the *Sánkhya-sára*, p. 17.

It were easy to enlarge on the peculiarities of these passages, and to point out many more cases of misapprehension in M. Saint-Hilaire's observations on the twenty-fifth *Káriká*.

on the Aphorisms of Patanjali. IV. The *Sánkhya-sára*, which awaits description. V. The *Yoga-sára-sangraha*, or *Jnána-pradípa*; a succinct exposition of the Yoga. Each of these works, from the last upwards, cites all that, as here disposed, precede it. But the *Sánkhya-bháshya* and the *Yoga-várttika* quote each other. Their author appears, accordingly, to have been engaged with both at the same time; unless he, or some one else, interpolated one or the other.

In all probability, Vijnána lived in the sixteenth or seventeenth century.* There is some slight ground, however, for carrying him back still further.† His nationality is unknown; and so is his civil appellation even: for Vijnána Bhikshu‡ is,

---

* According to an anecdote which I have heard from several pandits, Nágojí Bhaṭṭa, the epitomator of Vijnána's *Sánkhya-bháshya*, synchronized with Jayasinha, Rájá of Jaypur. The time of that prince is fixed by the fact, that, under him the *Jayasinha-kalpadruma*, by Ratnákara Bhaṭṭa, son of Deva Bhaṭṭa, was composed in the Samvat year 1770, or A. D. 1713. So much for oral tradition.

† In the *Prayoga-ratna*, a work on the sixteen sacraments, by Náráyaṇa Bhaṭṭa, son of Rámes'wara Bhaṭṭa, its author says, that he was assisted, in preparing it, by Ananta Díkshita, son of Vis'wanátha Díkshita. The father of one of Vijnána's disciples, Bhávágaṇes'a Díkshita, was Bhávávis'wanátha Díkshita; and, if the latter was one with Vis'wanátha Díkshita, and if Bhávágaṇes'a Díkshita was brother of Ananta Díkshita, we are enabled to form a pretty correct estimate as to the time of Vijnána Bhikshu. For Náráyaṇa Bhaṭṭa's youngest brother's second son, Raghunátha Bhaṭṭa, dates his *Kála-tattwa-vivechana* in Samvat 1677, or A. D. 1620. Vijnána may be placed fifty or sixty years earlier.

In the prefatory verses of Vijnána's *Pátanjala-bháshya-várttika*, according to one of the many MSS. of it which I have examined, reference is made to one Bhavadeva, as an authority on the Yoga. Bhavadeva Mis'ra, of Patna, author of the *Pátanjalíyábhinava-bháshya*, a commentary on the *Yoga-sútra*, seems to be intended. But of his age I know nothing.

‡ Or Vijnána Yati, as he is called just as often.

without question, the style of a devotee. Literature has preserved to us the names of three of his disciples :* Bhávágaṇes'a Díkshita,† Prasádamádhava Yogin,‡ and Divyasinha Mis'ra.§

The ignorance of our pandits very ordinarily confounds him with Vijnánes'wara, or Vijnána Yogin, author of the *Mitákshará*, the celebrated commentary on the *Yájnavalkya-smṛiti*. But there is no evidence whatever that they are identical. Vijnánes'wara, who bore the title of Bhaṭṭáraka, was son of Padmanábha Bhaṭṭa, of the stock of Bharadwája. His preceptor was Vis'warúpa A'chárya, likewise a scholiast of Yájnavalkya. Vis'warúpa A'chárya, it is said, was the same person as Sures'wara A'chárya, civilly called Maṇḍana Mis'ra; a disciple of S'ankara A'chárya.

* M. Saint-Hilaire says : "Un maître n'a généralement qu'un disciple; un gorou n'a qu'un brahmatchâri." *Premier Mémoire, &c.*, p. 7. Again : "La science, ainsi que j'ai eu occasion de le dire au début de ce mémoire, se transmet, dans l'Inde, habituellement d'un seul maître à un seul disciple." *Ibid.*, p. 254. This is news in India. Such cases no longer exist; and they must always have been exceptional.

† I have seen a MS., without date, of the *Tantra-chúḍamaṇi*, or *Dharma-mímánsá-sangraha*, an elementary Mímánsá disquisition, by Kṛishṇadeva, son of Ráma A'chárya, which professes to be in the hand-writing of that person. I incline to consider the age of the MS. to be, at the very least, a couple of centuries.

‡ Author of the *S'árira-káriká-bháshya*, or *Kárikártha-vinis'chaya*, a dissertation on the following enigmatical couplet, which its elucidator claims to take from the *Mahábhárata* :

एकया द्वे विनिश्चित्य त्रींश्चतुर्भिर्वशीकुरु ।
पञ्च जित्वा विदित्वा षट् सप्त हित्वा सुखी भव ॥

The dissertation is in four sections; one being allotted to each quarter of the distich.

§ Divyasinha Mis'ra has written a commentary, by name *S'árira-káriká-bháshya-várttika*, on the work mentioned in the last note. He styles himself fellow-student of Prasádamádhava Yogin, under Vijnána Bhikshu; and he eulogizes Prasádamádhava as the most eminent of their master's disciples.

The following is as complete a list as I am at present able to draw up, of works treating exclusively of the Sánkhya.

I. The *Sánkhya-káriká,** by I's'warakṛishṇa. Commentaries on it are:

A. The *Sánkhya-káriká-bháshya,* by Gauḍapáda, supposed to be one with the preceptor of Govinda, of whom S'ankara A'chárya was disciple.†

---

* I return to this work for a moment. Coupling it with th *Sánkhya-pravachana,* Colebrooke says, that both "may be considered to be genuine and authoritative expositions of the doctrine; and, the more especially, as they do not, upon any material point, appear to disagree." *Miscellaneous Essays,* Vol. I., p. 234.

On the subject of I's'wara, the *Sánkhya-pravachana* asserts, that there is no proof of his existence. May it not be, that I's'warakṛishṇa, since he avoids any such declaration, thought differently? Possibly he would have denied, that the Sánkhya, as he held it, even implicitly rejects I's'wara.

The original Sanskrit of the *Sánkhya-káriká,* unaccompanied by any commentary, has been published by Professor Lassen: also, in Roman characters, by M. G. Pauthier. These verses have been translated into Latin, by Professor Lassen; into German, by Dr. C. J. H. Windischmann; into English, by Colebrooke; and into French, by MM. G. Pauthier and Barthélemy Saint-Hilaire.

† See Colebrooke's *Miscellaneous Essays,* Vol. I., p. 233. S'ankara lived at "the close of the eighth, or beginning of the ninth, century." Id., *ibid.*, Vol. I., p. 332. Dr. F. H. H. Windischmann thinks, that he died not long before the year 750. *Sancara, sive de Theologumenis Vedanticorum,* p. 42.

The notion, that Gauḍapáda was pupil of S'uka, the son of Vyása, is generally received by the Bráhmans. See, for this association, Colebrooke's reference to the *S'ankara-digvijaya: Miscellaneous Essays,* Vol. I., p. 104.

Gangádhara Saraswatí, author of the *Dattátreya-charitra,* a metrical composition in the Maráthí language, deduces his own discipular descent, through S'uka and Gauḍapáda, from S'iva, as follows: S'ankara, Vishṇu, Brahmá, Vasishṭha, S'akti, Parás'ara, Vyása, S'uka,

B. The *Sánkhya-tattwa-kaumudí*, or *Sánkhya-kaumudí*, by Váchaspati Mis'ra, pupil of Mártaṇḍatilaka Swámin.* It has been annotated in

a. The *Tattwa-kaumudí-vyákhyá*, by Bháratí Yati, pupil of Bodha Áraṇya Yati.

Gauḍapáda Áchárya, Govinda Áchárya, S'ankara Áchárya, Vis'warúpa, Bodha Giri, Jnána Giri, Sinhála Giri, Ís'wara Tírtha, Nṛisinha Tírtha, Vidyá Tírtha, S'iva Tírtha, Bháratí Tírtha, Vidyá 'Áraṇya, S'rípáda, Vidyá Tírtha, Malaya Ánanda, Deva Tírtha, Vṛinda Saraswatí, Yádavendra Saraswatí, Kṛishṇa Saraswatí, Nṛisinha Saraswatí, and Gangádhara Saraswatí. Gangádhara had seven fellow-students, all bearing the title of Saraswatí : Bála, Kṛishṇa, Upendra, Mádhava, Sadánanda, Jnánajyoti, and Siddhendra.

The *Mitákshará*, a commentary on the *Brahma-sútra*, by Annam Bhaṭṭa, son of Tirumala, contains a list, identical, down to S'ankara Áchárya, with the foregoing; except that Vasishṭha is preceded by Brahma and Brahmá.

Gauḍapáda, it appears credible, belonged to the very precinct of the age of fable.

Gauḍapáda's scholia on the *Sánkhya-káriká*, including the memorial verses, were published, by Professor Wilson, at Oxford, in 1837. Prefixed to the originals is the Professor's translation of the scholia, accompanying Colebrooke's version of the text.

* The *Sánkhya-kaumudí* was published in Calcutta, in the *Samvat* year 1905, or A. D. 1848 : pp. 49, small 8vo.

Colebrooke—*Miscellaneous Essays*, Vol. I., p. 233,—seems to be of opinion, that the title of *Tattwa-kaumudí* is applied to Váchaspati's work only by comparatively recent abbreviation. But the concluding distich of the book itself, if not spurious, contains the shorter form. It also occurs in the list of Váchaspati's works, as detailed at the end of his *Bhámatí-nibandha;* and in Mádhava Áchárya's *Sarva-dars'ana-sangraha.*

Váchaspati's exact age has not yet been discovered. But he is mentioned, as are Udayana and Pras'astapáda, in the *Nyáya-sára-vichára* of Bhaṭṭa Rághava, which was written in the *S'aka* year 1174, or A. D. 1252; and he quotes from Bhoja, who was reigning in A. D. 1042.

b. The *Tattwárṇava*, or *Tattwámṛita-prakás'iní*, by Rághava Ánanda Saraswatí, disciple of Adwaya Ánanda, disciple of Vis'wes'wara.

c. The *Tattwa-chandra*,* by Náráyaṇa Tírtha, who studied under Vásudeva Tírtha and Rámagovinda Tírtha.

d. The *Kaumudí-prabhá*, by Swapnes'wara, son of Váhinís'a.

e. The *Sánkhya-tattwa-vilása*, *Sánkhya-vṛitti-prakás'a*, or *Sánkhyártha-sankhyáyika*, by Raghuṇátha Tarkavágís'a Bhaṭṭáchárya, son of S'ivaráma Chakravartin, son of Chandravandya, son of Kás'ínátha, son of Balabhadra, son of Sarvánanda Mis'ra. This is little more than a jejune epitome of the *Sánkhya-kaumudí*, with a preface briefly explaining the *Tattwa-samása*, which it repeats.

f. The *Sánkhya-tattwa-vibhákara*.†

C. The *Sánkhya-chandriká*, by Náráyaṇa Tírtha.

D. The *Sánkhya-kaumudí*, by Rámakṛishṇa Bhaṭṭáchárya, who is said to borrow freely from the author of the work last named.‡

II. The *Tattwa-samása*,§ expositions of which are:

---

* Of this work I have seen only a fragment of the beginning, going over Váchaspati's elucidation of the first eight *Káriká*s.

Two couplets, which appear in the *Sánkhya-pravachana-bháshya* as if by its author, are cited by Náráyaṇa. He may, then, have come after Vijnána Bhikshu.

† This work I know only from the first volume of Dr. Albrecht Weber's *Die Handschriften-Verzeichnisse der Königlichen Bibliothek*. Berlin: 1853, p. 638. Dr. Weber is in doubt whether its author's name be, or be not, Vans'ídhara.

‡ See Colebrooke's *Miscellaneous Essays*, Vol. I., p. 234. Rámakṛishṇa's work I have not seen. Professor Lassen—*Gymnosophista*: Pref. p. ix.,—makes it possible, that it bears the second title of *Sánkhya-sára*. Prof. Wilson leaves this point undiscussed. Oxford *Sánkhya-káriká*, Preface, p. vii.

§ Except for its having elicited comments that lay under contribution philosophical sources presumed to be no longer forthcom-

A. The *Sarvopakáriṇí*, by a nameless writer.

ing, the *Tattwa-samása* is of slight importance. It is a mere index to the topics of the Sánkhya.

The articles that make it up are variously reckoned by different authorities. The *Sarvopakáriṇí* counts but twenty-two; as follows: अष्टौ प्रकृतयः ॥ १ ॥ षोडश विकाराः ॥ २ ॥ पुरुषः ॥ ३ ॥ त्रैगुण्यसञ्चरः ॥ ४ ॥ प्रतिसञ्चरः ॥ ५ ॥ अध्यात्मम् ॥ ६ अधिभूतम् ॥ ७ ॥ अधिदैवतम् ॥ ८ ॥ पञ्चाभिबुद्धयः ॥ ९ ॥ पञ्च कर्मयोनयः ॥ १० ॥ पञ्च वायवः ॥ ११ ॥ पञ्च कर्मात्मानः ॥ १२ ॥ पञ्चपर्वाविद्या ॥ १३ ॥ अष्टाविंशतिधाशक्तिः ॥ १४ ॥ नवधा तुष्टिः ॥ १५ ॥ अष्टधा सिद्धिः ॥ १६ ॥ दश मूलिकार्थाः ॥ १७ ॥ अनुग्रहसर्गः ॥ १८ ॥ चतुर्दशविधो भूतसर्गः ॥ १९ ॥ त्रिविधो बन्धः ॥ २० ॥ त्रिविधो मोक्षः ॥ २१ ॥ त्रिविधं प्रमाणम् ॥ २२ ॥ एतद् याथातथ्यम्। एतत् सम्यग् ज्ञात्वा कृतकृत्यः स्यान् न पुनस्त्रिविधेन दुःखेनाऽभिभूयते।

The topic *traiguṇya-sanchara* is given as two, in all the other commentaries. It is only by this bisection, that the *Sánkhya-sútra-vivaraṇa* differs from the *Sarvopakáriṇí;* and thus exhibits twenty-three so-called *sútras.*

The *Sánkhya-krama-dípiká* recites, at its commencement, twenty-five topics, but clearly by error; as it reduces them to twenty-four, by foregoing all explication of the words *trividho dhátu-sargah,* which occur after the topic given above as the nineteenth. The MS. from which Dr. J. R. Ballantyne printed the work in question, seems to be peculiar in reading *trividho dhátu-sansargah.* In the preface to the *Sánkhya-tattwa-vilása,* where the *Tattwa-samása* is quoted, as if from the *Sánkhya-krama-dípiká,* and briefly elucidated, the expression *trividho dhátu-sargah* is explained by the words *váta-pitta-kapha-bhedát trividhah,* as intending the assemblage of wind, choler, and phlegm.

The *Sánkhya-krama-dípiká* gives after No. 22 as above, the words *trividham duhkham,* as a topic.

The reading of the *Tattwa-yáthárthya-dípana* corresponds with that of the *Sánkhya-krama-dípiká,* barring its rejection of *trividho,* &c., and its considering the words *etad yáthátathyam* as a topic; thus actually giving twenty-five as the total.

Kshemánanda, in his annotations on the *Tattwa-samása,* states, that it contains twenty-five topics: but he enumerates only twenty-four; his text being, as far as the words *etad yáthátathyam,* identical with that of the *Tattwa-yáthárthya-dípana.*

B. The *Sánkhya-sútra-vivaraṇa,* also by an anonymous author.

The eighth topic is read, in the *Sánkhya-sútra-vivaraṇa*, *adhidaivam cha ;* and *adhidaivatam cha*, in the *Sánkhya-krama-dípiká*, in the *Tattwa-yáthárthya-dípana*, and in Kshemánanda on the *Tattwa-samása.* The *Sarvopakáriṇí*, in its seventeenth topic, is unique in preferring *das'a* to *das'adhá.*

The *Tattwa-samása* is generally found appended to Vedánti Mahádeva's *Sánkhya-vṛitti-sára*, and according to the reading of the *Sarvopakáriṇí.* Mahádeva, however, perhaps for the sake of shortness, omits the two sentences by which the topics are usually followed.

Of the *Sánkhya-krama-dípiká* I have collated five MSS.

Another classification of the Sánkhya topics, which computes them at sixty, is propounded in the commentaries on the *Tattwa-samása*, and in the *Rája-várttika* as quoted in the *Sánkhya-kaumudí* and *Sarvopakáriṇí.* The passage from the *Rája-várttika* runs as follows:

प्रधानास्तित्वमेकत्वमर्थवत्त्वमथान्यता ।
पारार्थ्यं च तथानैक्यं वियोगो योग एव च ॥
शेषवृत्तिरकर्तृत्वं मौलिकार्थाः स्मृता दश ।
विपर्ययः पञ्चविधस्तथोक्ता नव तुष्टयः ॥
करणानामसामर्थ्यमष्टाविंशतिधा मतम् ।
इति षष्टिः पदार्थानामष्टाभिः सह सिद्धिभिः ॥

Professor Wilson—Oxford *Sánkhya-káriká*, pp. 191-2—completes, in some sort, the set of ten "radicals" here included; but only by copying Váchaspati where he supplements the text, and by misunderstanding him there and elsewhere. Váchaspati connects *astitwa* with both *purusha* and *prakṛiti ;* and yet in order to make but one category of the whole, Professor Wilson makes two: "existence of soul" and "existence of nature." Again, Váchaspati explains *s'esha-vṛitti*, by *sthiti*, which he refers to *sthúla* and *súkshma.* Professor Wilson, dividing, as before, gives two categories, "duration of subtile" and "that of gross." *Viyoga* and *yoga* are left, by Váchaspati, unexplained, as being too plain to demand elucidation. Prof. Wilson throws them out altogether.

In an anonymous marginal note to one of my MSS. of the *Sánkhya-káriká*, I have found the verses given above from the *Rája-*

C. The *Sánkhya-krama-dípiká, Sánkhyálankára,* or *Sánkhya-sútra-prakshepiká ;** likewise of unknown paternity.

D. The *Tattwa-yáṭhárthya-dípana,* by Bhávágaṇes'a Díkshita, son of Bhávávis'wanátha Díkshita, and pupil of Vijnána Bhikshu.

E. An unnamed volume of annotations, by Kshemánanda Díkshita,† son of Raghunandana Díkshita.

III. The *Sánkhya-pravachana,* on which but two regular commentaries have been ascertained as now extant:

A. The *Aniruddha-vṛitti,* by Aniruddha.‡

---

várttika, with the following stanza in place of their first couplet and a half:

पुरुषः प्रकृतिर्बुद्धिरहङ्कारो गुणास्त्रयः ।
तन्मात्रमिन्द्रियं भूतं मौलिकार्थाः स्मृता दश ॥

The commentaries on the *Taṭtwa-samása* cite the ensuing couplet for an enumeration of the ten radicals:

अस्तित्वमेकत्वमथार्थवत्त्वं पारार्थ्यमन्यत्वमकर्तृता च ।
योगो वियोगो बहवः पुमांसः स्थितिः शरीरस्य च शेषवृत्तिः ॥

The term *astitwa,* here used, is explained, by the other commentators, as it is by Váchaspati. *Vis'esha-vṛittih* is, in some MSS., substituted for *cha s'esha-vṛittih.* Its import is represented as above. See, regarding it, the sixty-seventh *Káriká* of I's'warakṛishṇa.

* This work was published and translated by Dr. J. R. Ballantyne, in 1850. Its titles were, at that time, unascertained.

Dr. Röer—*Journal of the Asiatic Society of Bengal,* for 1851, p. 405,—states, that the author of the *Sánkhya-tattwa-vilása* imputes this work to Ásuri; but he contests the credibility of the attribution, on the showing of the commentary itself. It does not positively appear, however, that the author of the *Sánkhya-tattwa-vilása* is speaking of the *Sánkhya-krama-dípiká.*

† The only copy I have inspected of Kshemánanda's notes on the *Tattwa-samása,* is imperfect in its latter half.

‡ Vijnána Bhikshu refers to him; and he is named in Rághava Ánanda's *Tattwárṇava.*

a. The *Sánkhya-vṛitti-sára*, by Mahádeva Saraswatí,* more commonly called Vedánti Mahádeva, disciple of Swayamprakás'a Tírtha, is an abridgment of Aniruddha, but contains many original remarks by the epitomist.

B. The *Sánkhya-pravachana-bháshya* or *Sánkhya-bháshya*, by Vijnána Bhikshu.†

---

* The *Gírváṇa-pada-manjarí* by Varadarája Bhaṭṭa, takes notice of a gloss on a *Sánkhya-bháshya*. In the opening couplets to many copies of the *Laghu-kaumudí*,—which was written in *Samvat* 1715, or A. D. 1658,—Varadarája is called pupil of Bhaṭṭojí Díkshita, and, as such, preceded Náges'a Bhaṭṭa by two generations. See Colebrooke's *Miscellaneous Essays*, Vol. II., pp. 12, 13. If, then, it be not Mahádeva's epitome which Varadarája intends, he probably refers to some work now lost.

† It was published by the editor of this volume, in 1854-1856, and forms Nos. 94, 97, and 141 of the *Bibliotheca Indica*. The oldest MS. used for it was dated in *Samvat* 1711, or A. D. 1654.

Dr. J. R. Ballantyne, in 1852-1856, published the *Sánkhya-pravachana*, with portions of commentary, and an English translation of both, in three volumes. As, in the last two, he has simply reprinted the Sanskrit as edited by me, some acknowledgment of obligation would not, perhaps, have been more than my due.

The first edition of the *Sánkhya-pravachana-bháshya* bears the imprint of Serampore, 1821: 8vo. pp. 220. This seems to be the publication announced as having been projected by "Mr. Carey and his assistants," under the auspices of the Council of Fort William, and the Asiatic Society of Bengal. See Captain Roebuck's *Annals of the College of Fort William*, p. 157. The faults of that impression need not now be made the subject of particularization. The editors of the volume had the advantage of a manuscript, or manuscripts, much superior to the use they made of their appliances.

The *Sánkhya-pravachana* contains 526 aphorisms, that is to say, in the six lectures, 164, 47, 84, 32, 129, and 70, respectively. As for this enumeration, even if it had not the support, by express declaration, of annotators, yet the tenor of their scholia would, n general, authorize it with sufficient distinctness. But it is expressly

a. The *Laghu-sán hya-sútra-vṛitti*, or *Laghu-sánkhya-vṛitti*, by Nágojí Bhaṭṭa, or Náges'a Bhaṭṭa Upádhyáya, is an abstract of the last.

---

supported, by notation, in all the copies of the pure text that I have consulted, and in most of the MSS. of Vijnána's commentary, and of Nágojí Bhaṭṭa's abstract of it, that I have collated. Anirudha, and his epitomist Mahádeva, of whose works such MSS. as I have examined likewise have the aphorisms numbered, concur, essentially, in the forementioned distribution and aggregate. The only difference which they discover consists in halving the 121st aphorism of Lecture V.; thus bringing out 527 as the sum total.

M. Saint-Hilaire—*Premier Mémoire sur le Sânkhya*, p. 6,—computes the Sánkhya aphorisms at 479; or 156, 46, 76, 30, 122, and 69. This came from his trusting, with a confidence not altogether scholarlike, the uncritical Serampore volume, which, with other faults, frequently gives text as commentary, and sometimes gives commentary as text. The consequence, to his essay, of neglecting due circumspection and research, is sufficiently disadvantageous. I add a couple of specimens.

Commenting on the fifty-fourth *Kârikâ*, M. Saint-Hilaire writes:

"Lecture 3, soûtra 44 [48]: 'En haut, il y a prédominance de la bonté.'

"Kapila ne va pas plus loin; et après avoir indiqué, comme on l'a vu, l'existence des trois mondes en n' indiquant que le monde des dieux où règne la bonté, il ne dit point quelle qualité prédomine dans les mondes qui viennent après celui-là. Il est probable que la Kârikâ, en faisant prédominer l'obscurité dans le monde inférieur, et le mal dans le monde du milieu, se conforme à une tradition dès longtemps reçue; mais, dans les axiomes du maître, ce complément à peu près indispensable de sa pensée n' apparaît pas, et il n'en a rien exprimé, pas même par une de ces réticences qui lui sont si habituelles. Il faut ajouter que le commentateur des Soûtras, Vidjnâna Bhikshou, ne s'est pas arrêté d'avantage à la doctrine que nous retrouvons dans la Kârikâ, et qu'à la suite de Kapila il a omis de parler des deux autres mondes, placés au-dessous du monde supérieur. Il se borne à dire que par 'en haut' Kapila comprend le monde qui est au-dessus de la terre habitée par les mortels." *Premier Mémoire*, &c., pp. 213, 214.

C. The *Sánkhya-taranga*, by Vis'wes'waradatta Mis'ra, or Deva Tírtha Swámin, but who was more generally known as

---

The restoration of III., 49 and 50, which, with the explanations of them, do not appear in the Serampore impression of Vijnána, at once accounts for several items of the fifty-fourth *Káriká*, and completely frustrates the criticism just quoted.

Again: "Colebrooke a fait remarquer (*Essays*, tom. I., page 232) que les Soûtras attribués à Kapila mentionnaient le nom de Pantchasikha. Le fait est exact, et Colebrooke en tirait cette double conséquence: d'abord, que les Soûtras n'étaient pas de Kapila lui-même, car il n'aurait pas cité le nom de son disciple; et, en second lieu, qu' il y avait pour le Sânkhya des autorités antérieures aux Soûtras, puisqu'ils invoquaient eux-mêmes le témoignage d'un maître plus ancien qu' eux. J' admets les deux conséquences signalées par Colebrooke. Mais il aurait dû ajouter que la citation rapportée par lui se trouve dans l'avant-dernier soûtra de tout le système. (Lecture 6, soûtra 68). A cette place, les interpolations ont été plus faciles certainement que dans le corps même de l'exposition, et il est fort possible qu'une main étrangère ait glissé celle-ci à la fin de l'ouvrage. Cette simple indication du nom de Pantchasikha ne nous apprend d'ailleurs absolument rien sur la vie de ce personnage; elle ne fait que consacrer le souvenir d'une de ses doctrines." *Premier Mémoire, &c.*, pp. 253, 254.

Now, in the first place, the suggestion broached by M. Saint-Hilaire, that VI., 68, as being the penultimate aphorism of the *Sánkhya-pravachana*, may, not improbably, be an interpolation, is weakened by the fact, that it is followed by two aphorisms instead of one; and his objection now lies, on his line of argument, more directly against the text commemorating Sanandana,—VI., 69,—which, in his reading of Vijnána, is consigned to the notes. Again, both he and Colebrooke failed to observe V., 32, which, likewise, in Vijnána, as received by the former, is simply a scantling of commentary.

The fact, that Panchas'ikha is mentioned in the *Sánkhya-pravachana*, fairly compels the alternative of rejecting all we read of his relation to Kapila, or of adopting the view, that Kapila was not the author of those sentences in their present shape. I cannot believe that he was. In point of style, for one thing, they have not, as I have before remarked, the slightest flavour of antiquity.

Vedánti Mahádeva, annotating V., 32, infers, simply from Pancha-s'ikha's name being given in the singular number, that the aphorist purposes to mark him as a separatist. The singular must, then, be taken to indicate, as compared with the plural, an inferior degree of respect. But Sanandana, though dignified with the title of *A'chárya*, is yet spoken of in the singular number. Mahádeva's words are: पञ्चशिख इत्येकवचनेन परमतमेतदिति सूचयति।

In the *Mahábhárata*, XII., 11875, Panchas'ikha is assigned to the family of Parás'ara; and the same poem, XII., 7895, speaks of his mother, Kapilá.

At XII., 7886, of the *Mahábhárata*, it is said:

यमाहुः कपिलं साङ्ख्याः परमर्षिं प्रजापतिम्।
स मन्ये तेन रूपेण विस्मापयति हि स्वयम्॥

"I can imagine, that he whom the Sánkhyas call Kapila, the mighty sage, the patriarch, is, in person, under this form, exciting our admiration."

Such is the unmistakable sense of the stanza; and so thinks Nílakaṇṭha Chaturdhara: स कपिलः। तेन पञ्चशिखरूपेण। तत्प्रशिष्यत्वात् तद्रूपत्वम्। Yet Professor Wilson understands the meaning to be, that Panchas'ikha is there "named .. .. Kapila." Oxford *Sánkhya-káriká*, p. 190. Dr. Weber repeats this mistake: "als auch Kapila heisst." *Indische Studien*, Vol. I., p. 433.

A Bangálí translation of the *Sánkhya-pravachana-bháshya*, entitled *Sánkhya-bháshá-sangraha*, was undertaken by Rámajaya Tarkálankára Bhaṭṭáchárya, son of Mṛityunjaya. So, at least, the work itself sets forth: but the *Friend of India* for 1823, No. VIII., p. 567, makes them to be joint translators, and adds, that they were, the last-named in succession to the other, "chief pandits in the Supreme Court." Mṛityunjaya, surnamed Vidyálankára, had previously been head-pandit in the College of Fort-William. This version conforms very closely to the Serampore edition of the original, from which, while still unpublished, it appears to have been prepared. How much of the translation was executed, or how much of it was printed, I am unable to say. All that I have seen of it is a fragment of 168

It is a fanciful performance, of slight extent, and of little value.*

IV. The *Rája-várttika*, complimentarily ascribed to Bhoja, King of Dhárá,† is, probably, a complete body of Sánkhya doctrine.

V. The *Sánkhya-sára*, by Vijnána Bhikshu, lays out the whole of the Sánkhya system within a small compass, and yet perspicuously.

VI. The *Sánkhya-tattwa-pradípa*, by Kavirája Yati, dis-

---

octavo pages, breaking off, abruptly, in the midst of the commentary on the eighty-ninth Aphorism of the first Lecture—according to my numbering. The volume was published at Serampore, in 1818. It opens with a short preface in Sanskrit; and it gives the *sútras* in the original language, and in large characters.

At Benares I have inspected a manuscript translation, in the provincial dialect, of the *Sánkhya-pravachana* and of Vijnána's exposition in abstract. The author was Áhitágni Rakshapála Dúbe; who also showed me Hindí versions, made by himself, on a like model, of the Yoga, Nyáya, Vais'eshika, Vedánta, and Mímánsá Aphorisms, and of S'áṇḍilya's Sentences on Devotion. Each of the translations was accompanied, like that of the *Sánkhya-pravachana*, by a Hindí gloss, abridged from the Sanskrit.

* Its author owed his epithet to his wearing a cleft stick on his tongue, during the latter years of his life, as a check on loquacity. Vis'wes'waradatta died at Benares about ten years ago. His preceptor was one Vidyá Áraṇya Tírtha, a Sáraswata Bráhman. The *Sánkhya-taranga* belongs to a series of tracts called, collectively, *S'rí-kás'í-rája-ságara*. I have seen at least twelve or fifteen works by its author, who composed largely in Hindí and Maráthí, no less than in Sanskrit.

† For this appropriation I am indebted to the learned Pandit Kás'ínátha S'ástrí Ashṭaputre, late of the Benares College. The Pandit is by far too well acquainted with Bhoja's commentary on the *Yoga-sútra*, to have mistaken it for the *Rája-várttika*. The latter treatise, he assures me, was in his possession for several years, during which he constantly lectured on it to his pupils.

ciple of Vaikuṇṭha, is a composition of similar scope, but of inferior value.

VII. The *Sánkhyártha-tattwa-pradípiká,* by Bhaṭṭa Kes'ava, son of Sadánanda, son of Bhaṭṭa Kes'ava, resembles the last, and is not a work of much account.*

In the *Sánkhya-sára* we have the best known existing treatise in which to study the system ascribed to Kapila. This treatise consists of two sections, in prose and in verse, respectively. The first section is in three chapters, treating of emancipation as the fruit of discriminative apprehension, of the character of such apprehension, and of that from which spirit is to be discriminated.† The second section contains seven chapters, explanatory of the nature of spirit, of the

---

* Colebrooke speaks of a work entitled *Sangraha,* having to do with the Sánkhya. I do not recall having met, in the course of my researches, with any reference to it. See *Miscellanous Essays,* Vol. I., p. 234.

The *Sánkhya-muktávali,* by Voḍhu, is the name of a Sánkhya work possibly now, or once, in existence; if the bare word of a man who has declared to me, that he once possessed and perused a copy of it, is to be received. But I strongly suspect that he fabricated the title of the treatise, for the occasion.

Mr. William Ward has published a list of Sánkhya compositions, in his work on the Hindus; Vol. II., p. 121: 8vo. ed. of 1822. That list is, however, one mass of errors, and errrors almost too gross to deserve advertence. It assigns the *Kapila-bháshya* to Vis'wes'warí, perhaps instead of Vijnánes'wara, as one sometimes hears Vijnána Bhikshu incorrectly called; while it speaks of the *Sánkhya-pravachana-bháshya* as a distinct composition, and neglects to name its author. Váchaspati Mis'ra's *Sánkhya-kaumudí* is, in like manner, duplicated. This for a sample.

† In that chapter, the third, there is much about the term *guṇa.* At p. 6, *supra,* a note on the subject has been promised; but, for the present, it must be postponed. In the meantime, the reader is referred to my translation of Pandit Nehemiah Níḷakaṇṭha's *Rational Refutation,* &c., pp. 42, etc.

distinction between spirit and what is not spirit, of coercion of the mind, of emancipation in the body,* and of supreme emancipation.

But for my being on the point of leaving India, with no thought of returning, I should append to this preface a full translation of the *Sánkhya-sára*, accompanied by annotations.†

The following pages were printed from two undated manuscripts. One of them I procured at Benares; and the other belongs to the Asiatic Society of Bengal. For the readings of the latter, I have to thank Mr. Cowell, the Society's Secretary. Though I spared no pains in the quest, no other manuscripts but those I have used were obtainable; and my text, I am well aware, is not immaculate.

Camp Tappá,
State of Gwalior,
March 15, 1862.

---

* Colebrooke represents the *Sánkhya-sára* as being a "treatise on the attainment of beatitude in this life." *Miscellaneous Essays*, Vol. I., p. 231. That topic is one of two to which its concluding chapter only is devoted.

† Mr. Ward's version of the *Sánkhya-sára*, with all its imperfections, is of some value. It will be found in his work on the Hindus, Vol. II., pp. 121-172 of the octavo edition printed in 1822.

साङ्ख्यसारः ।

श्रीयुतेन फित्स-एड्वार्ड्-हल-नामकमहोदयेन

प्रकाशितः ।

कलिकातानगरे

बाप्तिष्ट-मिशन्-यन्त्रे ग्रन्थोऽयं मुद्राङ्कितोऽभूत् ।

शकाब्दाः १७८६ । इं० १८६५ ।

साङ्ख्यसारः ।

पूर्वभागः ।

प्रथमः परिच्छेदः ।

मच्छदाख्यः स्वयम्भूर्यो जगदङ्कुर ईश्वरः ।
सर्वात्मने नमस्तस्मै विष्णवे सर्वजिष्णवे ॥ १ ॥
साङ्ख्यकारिकया लेशादात्मतत्त्वं विवेचितम् ।
साङ्ख्यसारविवेकोऽतो विज्ञानेन प्रपञ्च्यते ॥ २ ॥
प्रायः सङ्कलिता साङ्ख्यप्रक्रिया कारिकागणे ।
साऽतोऽत्र वर्ण्यते लेशात् तदनुक्तांशमात्रतः ॥ ३ ॥
साङ्ख्यभाष्ये प्रकृत्यादेः स्वरूपं विस्तरान् मया ।
प्रोक्तं तस्मात् तदप्यत्र सङ्क्षेपादेव वक्ष्यते ॥ ४ ॥

आत्मानात्मविवेकसाक्षात्कारात् कर्तृत्वाद्यखिलाभिमान-निवृत्त्या तत्कार्यरागद्वेषधर्माधर्माद्यनुत्पादात् पूर्वोत्पन्नकर्मणां चाऽविद्यारागादिसहकार्युच्छेदरूपदाहेन विपाकानारम्भक-त्वात् प्रारब्धसमाप्त्यनन्तरं पुनर्जन्माभावेन त्रिविधदुःखा-

त्यन्तनिवृत्तिरूपो मोक्षो भवतीतिश्रुतिस्मृतिडिण्डिमः । तत्र श्रुतयः । अथाऽकामयमानो योऽकामो निष्कामो न तस्य प्राणा उत्क्रामन्तीहैव समवलीयन्ते ।

आत्मानं चेद् विजानीयादयमस्मीति पूरुषः ।
किमिच्छन् कस्य कामाय शरीरमनुसञ्ज्वरेत् ॥
यदा सर्वे प्रमुच्यन्ते कामा येऽस्य हृदि श्रिताः ।
अथ मर्त्योऽमृतो भवत्यत्र ब्रह्म समश्नुते ॥

कामान् यः कामयते मन्यमानः
स कर्मभिर्जायते तत्र तत्र ।
पर्याप्तकामस्य कृतात्मनस्तु
इहैव सर्वे प्रविलीयन्ति कामाः ॥

इत्याद्याः । स्मृतयश्च कौर्माद्याः । यथा कौर्मे ।

रागद्वेषादयो दोषाः सर्वे भ्रान्तिनिबन्धनाः ।
कार्यो ह्यस्य भवेद् दोषः पुण्यापुण्यमिति श्रुतिः ॥
तद्वशादेव सर्वेषां सर्वदेहसमुद्भवः ।

इति । मोक्षधर्मे च ।

इन्द्रियाणीन्द्रियार्थाश्च नोपसर्पन्त्यतर्षुलम् ।
हीनश्च करणैर्देही न देहं पुनरर्हति ॥
तस्मात् तर्षात्मकाद् रागाद् बीजाज् जायन्ति जन्तवः ।

इति । ननु रागाभावेऽपि केवलकर्मवशान् नरकादिप्राप्तेः कथं रागस्य कर्मसहकारित्वं विपाकारम्भ उपपन्नम् । नरकादौ विशेषतो रागाभावेऽपि सामान्यतो रागसत्त्वात् ।

निषिद्धस्त्र्यादिगामिना स्त्र्यादिरागादेव तप्तलोहमयनारीसमालिङ्गनादिरूपनरकोत्पत्तेः। यद्यप्यविद्यास्मितारागद्वेषभयाख्यं क्लेशपञ्चकमेव जन्मादिविपाकारम्भे कर्मणां सहकारि भवति।

तदेव सक्तः सह कर्मणैति
लिङ्गं मनो यत्र निषक्तमस्य।

इति श्रुतावभिमानरागद्वेषादिजन्यस्य विषयवासनाख्यसङ्गसामान्यस्यैव जन्मादिविपाकारम्भे कर्मसहकारित्वसिद्धेः।

यत्र यत्र मनो देही धारयेत् सकलं धिया।
स्नेहाद् द्वेषाद् भयाद् वाऽपि याति तत्तत्स्वरूपताम्॥

इत्यादिस्मृतेश्च। तथा च क्लेशमूलः कर्माशयः। सति मूले तद्विपाको जात्यायुर्भोगा इति योगसूत्राभ्यामप्यदृष्टे तद्विपाकारम्भे च क्लेशानां हेतुत्ववचनाच् च। तथाऽप्यविद्यास्मितासत्त्वे रागस्याऽऽवश्यकत्वाद् द्वेषभययोश्च रागमूलकत्वाद् राग एव मुख्यतो जन्मादिहेतुतया यथोक्तवाक्यैर्निर्दिश्यत इति। ननु।

क्षीयन्ते चाऽस्य कर्माणि तस्मिन् दृष्टे परावरे।

इत्यादिश्रुतेर्ज्ञानस्य प्राचीनकर्मनाशकत्वमेवोचितं दाहकत्वं कथमिष्यत इति चेन् न।

ज्ञानाग्निदग्धकर्माणं तमाहुः पण्डितं बुधाः।

इत्यादिवाक्यैर्दाहस्याऽपि श्रवणेन लाघवाद् दाहपरत्वस्यैव नाशादिवाक्येष्वपि कल्पनौचित्यात्। कर्मणां दाहश्च क्लेशाख्य-

सहकार्युच्छेदेन नैष्फल्यम् । कर्मणां नाशस्तु प्रारब्धभोगान्ते चित्तनाशादेव भविष्यति । अतो लोकसिद्धेनाऽविद्यानाशेनैव द्वारेण कर्मफलानुत्पत्तिसम्भवान् न ज्ञानस्य कर्मनाशकत्वं गौरवादित्यादिकं योगवार्त्तिके प्रपञ्चितमस्माभिरिति दिक् । तस्माद् विवेकसाक्षात्कारादविद्यास्मितारागादिक्लेशनिवृत्तौ त्रिविधदुःखात्यन्तनिवृत्तिरूपपरमपुरुषार्थः सिध्यतीत्युपपन्नम् । तथा च योगसूत्रद्वयम् । हेयं दुःखमनागतम् । विवेकख्यातिरविप्लवा हानोपाय इति ।

इति श्रीविज्ञानभिक्षुविरचिते साङ्ख्यसारेऽभ्यर्हितत्वादादौ विवेकख्यातिफलस्य परमपुरुषार्थस्य परिच्छेदः ॥ १ ॥

अथ द्वितीयः परिच्छेदः ।

अथाऽऽत्मानात्मविवेकज्ञानस्य किं स्वरूपं तदुच्यते। आत्मा तावत् सुखदुःखाद्यनुभवितेति सामान्यतो लोकप्रसिद्धिः अनात्मा च प्रकृत्यादिर्जडवर्गः तयोरन्योन्यवैधर्म्येण परिणामित्वापरिणामित्वादिरूपेण दोषगुणात्मकेन हेयोपादेयतया पृथक्त्वेन ज्ञानं विवेकज्ञानम्। तथा च श्रुतिः। स एष नेति नेत्यात्माऽगृह्यो न हि गृह्यतेऽशीर्यो न हि शीर्यतेऽसङ्गो न हि सज्यतेऽसितो न व्यथते न रिष्यतीत्यादि। स्मृतिश्च।

सोऽथ प्रतिनिवृत्ताक्षो गुरुदर्पणबोधितः।
स्वतोऽन्यां विक्रियां मौढ्यादास्थितामभ्यसैक्षत॥
अथाऽसौ प्रकृतिर्नीचमियं हि कलुषात्मिका।
शुद्धबुद्धस्वभावोऽहमिति त्यजति तां विदन्॥
एवं देहेन्द्रियादिभ्यः शुद्धत्वेनाऽऽत्मनि स्मृते।
निखिला सविकारेयं त्यक्तप्रायाऽहिचर्मवत्॥

इति। सूत्रं च। एवं तत्त्वाभ्यासान् नेति नेतीतित्यागाद् विवेकसिद्धिरिति। तत्त्वज्ञानस्य लक्षणं च मात्स्ये कृतम्।

अव्यक्ताद्ये विशेषान्ते विकारेऽस्मिंश्च वर्णिते।
चेतनाचेतनान्यत्वज्ञानेन ज्ञानमुच्यते॥

इति। यद्यप्यन्योन्यभेदज्ञानमेव विवेकज्ञानं तथाऽप्यात्मविशेष्यकमेव तन्मोक्षकारणं भवति। आत्मा वाऽरे द्रष्टव्य इत्यादिश्रुतिस्मृतिभ्यः। नन्वनात्मन्यात्मबुद्धिरूपा याऽविद्या

पातञ्जलादिषूक्ता तस्याः कथमात्मविशेष्यकविवेकज्ञानना-श्यत्वं प्रकारादिभेदादिति चेन् न। तादृश्याविद्याया अनात्मविशेष्यकविवेकज्ञानद्वारेणाऽऽत्मविशेष्यकविवेकज्ञाननाश्यत्वादिति। यच्च योगेन निर्विकल्पकमात्मज्ञानं जायते तद् विवेकज्ञानद्वारैव मोक्षकारणं भवति न तु साक्षादविद्यानिवर्तकत्वाभावात्। अहं गौरः कर्ता सुखी दुःखीत्यादिज्ञानमेव ह्यविद्या संसारानर्थहेतुतया श्रुतिस्मृतिन्यायसिद्धा तस्याश्च निवर्तिका नाऽहं गौर इत्यादिरूपा विवेकख्यातिरेव भवति। समाने विषये ग्राह्याभावत्वप्रकारकग्राह्याभावज्ञानत्वेनैव विरोधात्। अन्यथा शुक्तिनिर्विकल्पकस्याऽपि इदं रजतमिति ज्ञानविरोधित्वापत्तेः। किञ्च यथोक्ताभावज्ञाने ग्राह्यज्ञानविरोधित्वस्याऽऽवश्यकतया निर्विकल्पकज्ञानस्य भ्रमनिवर्तकत्वं न पृथक् कल्प्यते गौरवात्। अपि चाऽथाऽत आदेशो नेति नेति न ह्येतस्मादिति नेत्यन्यत् परमस्तीत्यादिश्रुत्या विवेकोपदेशापेक्षयोत्तमोपदेशो नाऽस्तीत्युच्यते।

क्षेत्रक्षेत्रज्ञयोरेवमन्तरं ज्ञानचक्षुषा।
भूतप्रकृतिमोक्षं च ये विदुर्यान्ति ते परम्॥

इति गीतादिवाक्यैश्च विवेकज्ञानस्यैव मोक्षहेतुत्वमुच्यते। अतो विवेकज्ञानमेव साक्षादविद्यानिवृत्त्या मोक्षहेतुः। योगेन केवलात्मसाक्षात्कारस्तु योग्यानुपलब्धिविधयोपाध्यादिगतधर्माभावमुपाध्यादिभेदं च ग्राहयति ततोऽविद्यानिवृत्तिरिति। एतेन सर्वभूतेषु समताज्ञानमात्मनः सर्वा-

त्मकत्वादिज्ञानं च श्रुतिस्मृत्योर्गीयमानं विवेकज्ञानस्यैव शेषभूतं सर्वदर्शनेषु मन्तव्यम्। ज्ञानान्तराणां साक्षादभिमानानिवर्तकत्वात्। ब्रह्ममीमांसायां त्वयं विशेषो यत् परमात्मविवेकशेषत्वम्। साङ्ख्यशास्त्रे तु सामान्यात्मविवेकशेषत्वमिति दिक्। ननु यथोक्तविवेकख्यातितोऽप्यत्यन्तमविद्योच्छेदो न घटते। विवेकख्यातेरविद्याप्रतिबन्धकत्वमात्रत्वेन विवेकख्यातिनाशोत्तरं पुनरभिमानसम्भवात्। शुक्तिरजतविवेकदर्शिनोऽपि कालान्तरे शुक्तौ रजतभ्रमवदिति। मैवम्। दृष्टान्तवैषम्यात्। शुक्त्यादिषु जातेऽपि साक्षात्कारे दूरत्वादिरूपविषयदोषाणां पटलादिरूपकरणदोषाणां चोत्पत्तिसम्भवेन पुनर्भ्रमो युक्तः। अनात्मन्यात्माभिमाने त्वनादिवासनैव दोषः सर्वास्तिकसम्मतः आत्ममात्रस्याऽभिमाने दोषान्तरानुपलब्धेः। सा मिथ्याज्ञानवासना यदा विवेकख्यातिपरम्पराजन्यदृढवासनोन्मूलिता तदैव विवेकसाक्षात्कारनिष्ठोच्यते। तत्पूर्वमवश्यं वासनालेशतो मिथ्यांशस्य कस्याऽप्यात्मनि भावात् तस्यां च विवेकख्यातिनिष्ठायां जातायां न पुनरभिमानः सम्भवति वासनाख्यदोषाभावादिति तु महद् वैषम्यम्। यदि तु बुद्धिपुरुषयोरन्योन्यप्रतिबिम्बनादिकमविवेककारणं दोष इष्यते तदा तु तद्दोषं बाधित्वैव विवेकसाक्षात्कार उदित इति न तस्य पुनर्भ्रमहेतुत्वं फलबलेन योगजधर्मसहकृतस्यैव तस्य दोषत्वकल्पनासम्भवादिति। विवेकख्यातिनिष्ठा च गीतादिषु लक्षिता।

प्रकाशं च प्रवृत्तिं च मोहमेव च पाण्डव ।
न द्वेष्टि सम्प्रवृत्तानि न निवृत्तानि काङ्क्षति ॥
उदासीनवदासीनो गुणैर्यो न विचाल्यते ।
सर्वारम्भपरित्यागी गुणातीतः स उच्यते ॥

इति । गुणातीतो निवृत्तगुणाभिमानः । अधिकं तु ज्ञानिलक्षणमग्रे वक्ष्यामः । नन्वेवमपि विवेकप्रतियोगिपदार्थानामानन्त्येन प्रातिस्विकरूपैः सर्वपदार्थेभ्यो विवेकग्रहासम्भवात् कथं विवेकख्यातेर्मोक्षहेतुत्वमिति चेन् न । दृश्यत्वपरिणामित्वादिसामान्यरूपैर्विवेकग्रहसम्भवात् । तथा हि । द्रष्टा स्वसाक्षात्प्रकाश्येभ्यो भिन्नः प्रकाशकत्वाद् यो यस्य प्रकाशकः स तस्माद् भिन्नः यथा घटादालोको वृत्तिप्रकाश्याच् च वृत्तिरित्यनुमानेनाऽऽदावन्तर्दृश्येभ्यो बुद्धिवृत्तितदारूढार्थेभ्यो विवेकतो बुद्धिसाक्षी सिध्यति । कर्मकर्तृविरोधश्चाऽनुकूलस्तर्कः । अत्र आत्मनि व्यभिचारवारणाय साक्षात्पदम् । वृत्तिद्वारैवाऽऽत्मनः स्वविषयत्वात् । नन्वत्राऽनुमाने बुद्धिवृत्तिमात्राद् विवेकः सिध्यतु । तस्या एव साक्षादात्मदृश्यत्वात् न प्रकृत्यादिभ्य इति चेन् न । वृत्तीनामज्ञातसत्त्वाभावेन ह्यत्राऽनुमाने लाघवाद् वक्ष्यमाणतर्कगणाच् चाऽखिलवृत्तीनां द्रष्टा विभुकूटस्थनित्यैकज्ञानस्वरूपतयैव सिध्यति । यथा नैयायिकानां क्षितिः सकर्तृका कार्यत्वादित्यनुमाने लाघवात् कर्तुरेकत्वनित्यत्वादिकं तद्वत् । तत्र विभुत्वं परिच्छिन्नभिन्नत्वं कूटस्थत्वादिकत्वं च परिणामिभिन्नत्वादिकमतो बुद्ध्या-

त्मनोर्दृग्दृश्यरूपतो विवेकग्रहे सति तदुत्तरानुमानेन परिणामित्वापरिणामित्वादिरूपैः सामान्यतोऽप्यात्मानात्मविवेकग्रहो घटत इति। अतएव पातञ्जले सत्त्वपुरुषान्यताख्यातिरेव मोक्षहेतुतया स्थले स्थले व्यासभाष्ये प्रोक्ता। सत्त्वपुरुषान्यताख्यातिरूपदृग्दृश्यविवेकग्रहोत्तरं यथोक्तरीत्या प्रकृत्यादिविवेकग्रहात्। तत्र च सत्त्वशब्दे बुद्धिस्थत्वेन बुद्धिसत्त्वमुक्तमिति। एवं च प्रकृत्यादिपदार्थानां विशिष्यज्ञानाभावेऽपि तद्विवेकज्ञानं घटते। एतेन दृग्दृश्यविवेकादविद्यानिवृत्तिरिति प्राचां प्रवादोऽप्युपपादितः। किञ्चाऽऽत्मा प्रकृतितत्कार्येभ्यो भिन्नोऽपरिणामित्वादित्याद्यनुमानैरपि सामान्यतो दृश्यविवेको द्रष्टरि सम्भवतीति। यत् त्वाधुनिका वेदान्तिब्रुवा दृश्यत्वेनैव प्रकृत्यादीनां द्रष्टृत्वेन च प्रकृत्याद्यखिलजडेभ्य आत्मविवेकं मन्यन्ते।

घटद्रष्टा घटाद्भिन्नः सर्वथा न घटो यथा।
देहद्रष्टा तथा देहो नाऽहमित्यादिरूपतः॥

तन् न। आत्मा वाऽरे द्रष्टव्य इत्यादिश्रुतिभिरात्मनोऽपि दृश्यत्वात् साक्षाद् दृश्यत्वविवक्षया च प्रकृत्यादेरसङ्ग्रहात् करणद्वारैव तद्दर्शनात्। अथैवं कल्पनीयं आत्मनो वृत्तिव्याप्यत्वमेव दृश्यत्वं श्रुत्यादिभिर्विधीयते न तु प्रकाश्यत्वरूपफलव्याप्यत्वम्। स्वयम्प्रकाशस्वरूपस्य प्रकाशापेक्षाविरहात्। अतोऽत्र दृश्यत्वं प्रकाश्यत्वं तच् चाऽऽत्मनि नाऽस्तीति तदपि तुच्छम्। यथा ह्यहमित्यनुभूयमानोऽप्यात्मा चैत-

न्याख्यफलव्याप्यो न भवतीति भवद्भिरुच्यते तथैव बौद्धैरपीष्यते सुखदुःखादिमत्त्वेनाऽपि बुद्धिः स्वप्रकाशतया चैतन्यव्याप्या न भवतीति । तथा चाऽऽत्मनीव बुद्धावपि दृश्यत्वासिद्ध्या दृश्यत्वेन रूपेण बुद्धिविवेकोऽत्यन्तापेक्षितोऽपि न सिध्यतीति भाष्यादिषु चाऽन्यान्यत्र दूषणान्युक्तानीति दिक् । ननु सम्भवत्वेवं सामान्यरूपेण विवेकग्रहः । तथाऽपि सामान्यान्येव बहूनि सन्ति परिणामित्वसंहत्यकारित्वसुखदुःखमोहात्मकत्वचतुर्विंशतितत्त्वत्वादीन्यतस्तैस्तै रूपैर्विवेकग्रहाणां मोक्षहेतुत्वेऽननुगमदोष इति चेन् न । अभिमानप्रतिबन्धकज्ञानत्वेनैवाऽनुगमादिति । अथैवं सामान्यरूपेण विवेकस्यैव सर्वाभिमाननिवर्तकतया नाऽहं देहो नेन्द्रियाणीत्यादिप्रत्येकरूपैर्विवेकग्रहाणां मोक्षहेतुत्वं श्रुतिस्मृत्योरुच्यमानं कथं घटतेति चेन् न । अवान्तरविवेकानां सामान्यविवेकप्रपञ्चमात्रत्वादिति ॥

इति श्रीविज्ञानभिक्षुविरचिते साङ्ख्यसारे मोक्षहेतुविवेकज्ञानस्य स्वरूपस्य परिच्छेदः ॥ * ॥

अथ तृतीयः परिच्छेदः ।

अथ के ते प्रकृत्यादयो येभ्यः पुरुषो विवेचनीय इत्युच्यते।

प्रकृतिर्बुद्ध्यहङ्कारौ तन्मात्रैकादशेन्द्रियम् ।
भूतानि चेति सामान्याच् चतुर्विंशतिरेव ते ॥

एतेष्वेव धर्मधर्म्यभेदेन गुणकर्मसामान्यानामन्तर्भावः। तत्र प्रकृतित्वं साक्षात् परम्परयाऽखिलविकारोपादानत्वं प्रकरोति इति प्रकृतिः परिणामरूपाऽस्या इति व्युत्पत्तेः। प्रकृतिः शक्तिरजा प्रधानमव्यक्तं तमो मायाऽविद्येत्यादयः प्रकृतेः पर्यायाः।

आप्नोति विद्याऽविद्येति मायेति च तथा परे ।
प्रकृतिश्च परा चेति वदन्ति परमर्षयः ॥

इति स्मृतेः। सा च साम्यावस्थयोपलक्षितं सत्त्वादिद्रव्यचयम्। कार्यसत्त्वादिवारणायोपलक्षितान्तम्। साम्यावस्था च न्यूनाधिकभावेनाऽसंहननावस्था अकार्यावस्थेति यावत्। महदादिकं तु कार्यसत्त्वादिकं न कदाऽप्यकार्यावस्थं भवतीति तद्व्यावृत्तिः। वैषम्यावस्थायामपि प्रकृतित्वसिद्धय उपलक्षितमित्युक्तम्। अकार्यमिति तूपलक्षितान्तस्य निष्कृष्टार्थः। सत्त्वादिगुणवती सत्त्वाद्यतिरिक्ता प्रकृतिरिति न शङ्कनीयम्। सत्त्वादीनामतद्धर्मत्वं तद्रूपत्वादिति साङ्ख्यसूत्रेण सत्त्वादीनां प्रकृतिस्वरूपत्वहेतुना प्रकृतिधर्मत्वप्रतिषेधात्। योगसूत्रतद्भाष्याभ्यामपि गुणानामेव प्रकृतित्ववचनाच् च। गुणेभ्य एव

कार्योत्पत्तौ तदन्यप्रकृतिकल्पनावैयर्थ्याच्च च। प्रकृतेर्गुणा इत्यादिवाक्यं तु वनस्य वृक्षा इतिवद् बोध्यम्।

सत्त्वं रजस्तम इति प्रकृतेरभवन् गुणाः।

इति सत्त्वादीनां प्रकृतिकार्यत्ववचनं तु गुणनित्यतावाक्यविरोधेन महत्तत्त्वकारणीभूतकार्यसत्त्वादिपरमेव। महदादिसृष्टिर्हि गुणवैषम्यात् श्रूयते। तच्च च वैषम्यं सजातीयसवलनेन गुणान्तरव्यावृत्तप्रकाशादिफलोपहितः सत्त्वादिव्यवहारयोग्यः परिणाम इति। एतेनाऽष्टाविंशतितत्त्वपक्षोऽप्युपपादितो मन्तव्यः। वैषम्य एव सत्त्वादिव्यवहारस्य श्रुतौ दृश्यते। यथा तम एवेदमग्र आस तत्परेणेरितं विषमत्वं प्रयात्येतद् वै रजसो रूपं तद्रजः खल्वीरितं विषमत्वं प्रयात्येतद् वै सत्त्वस्य रूपमिति। सत्त्वादित्रयं च सुखप्रकाशलाघवप्रसादादिगुणवत्तया संयोगविभागादिमत्तयाऽनाश्रितत्वोपादानत्वादिना च द्रव्यत्वेऽपि पुरुषोपकरणत्वात् पुरुषबन्धकत्वाच्च च गुणशब्देनोच्यते। इन्द्रियादिवत्। गुणानां सुखदुःखमोहात्मकत्वप्रवादस्तु धर्मधर्म्यभेदात्। मनसः सङ्कल्पात्मकत्ववत्। तत्र सत्त्वं सुखप्रसादप्रकाशाद्यनेकधर्मकं प्राधान्यतस्तु सुखात्मकमुच्यते। एवं रजोऽपि दुःखकालुष्यप्रवृत्त्याद्यनेकधर्मकं प्राधान्यतस्तु दुःखात्मकमुच्यते। तथा तमोऽपि मोहावरणस्तम्भनाद्यनेकधर्मकं प्राधान्यतस्तु मोहात्मकमुच्यते। त एव धर्मास्तेषां लक्षणानि भवन्ति। सत्त्वादिसञ्ज्ञा चाऽन्वर्था। सतो भावः सत्त्वमुत्तमत्वमिति व्युत्पत्त्या

हि धर्मप्राधान्येनोत्तमं पुरुषोपकरणं सत्त्वशब्दार्थः। मध्यमं च रजःशब्दार्थो रागयोगात्। अधमं च तमःशब्दार्थः। अधर्मावरणयोगात्। तानि च सत्त्वादीनि प्रत्येकमसङ्ख्यव्यक्तयः। लघुत्वादिधर्मैरन्योन्यसाधर्म्यं वैधर्म्यं च गुणानामिति साङ्ख्यसूत्रात्। अत्र हि सूत्रे लघुत्वादिना बहूनां सत्त्वानां साधर्म्यं तेनैव रजस्तमोभ्यां वैधर्म्यम्। एवं चलत्वादिना गुरुत्वादिना च बहूनां रजसां बहूनां च तमसां तदुभयमुक्तमिति। किञ्च यदि सत्त्वादित्रयमेकैकव्यक्तिरेव स्यात् तत् त्रयं विभ्वेव वक्तव्यम्। एकदाऽनेकब्रह्माण्डादिसृष्टिश्रवणात्। तथा च कार्याणामनन्तवैचित्र्यं न घटते। न च संयोगवैचित्र्याद् वैचित्र्यं स्यादिति वाच्यम्। विभूनां त्रयाणां गुणानां स्वतः संयोगवैचित्र्यासम्भवात्। द्रव्यान्तरस्य चाऽवच्छेदकीभूतस्याऽभावादिति। तस्मात् सत्त्वादीन्यसङ्ख्यव्यक्तिकान्येव द्रव्याणि। तेषु त्रित्ववचनं तु सत्त्वत्वादिविभाजकोपाधित्रयेण वैशेषिकाणां नवद्रव्यवचनवदिति सिद्धम्। तानि च सत्त्वादीनि यथायोग्यमणुविभुपरिमाणकानि। अन्यथा रजसश्चलस्वभावत्ववचनविरोधात्। आकाशकारणत्वस्य च विभुत्वौचित्यात्। सर्वेषां कारणद्रव्याणां विभुत्वे कार्याणां परिच्छिन्नत्वानुपपत्तेश्च। नन्वेवं वैशेषिकोक्तान्येव पार्थिवाण्वादीनि प्रकृतिरित्यायातमिति चेन् न। गन्धादिगुणशून्यत्वेन कारणद्रव्येषु पृथिवीत्वाद्यभावतोऽस्माकं विशेषात्। तदुक्तं विष्णुपुराणादिषु॥

अव्यक्तं कारणं यत् तत् प्रधानमृषिसत्तमैः।

प्रोच्यते प्रकृतिः सूक्ष्मा नित्यं सदसदात्मकम्॥
शब्दस्पर्शविहीनं तद् रूपादिभिरसंयुतम्।
त्रिगुणं तज् जगद्योनिरनादिप्रभवाप्ययम्॥

इत्यादिना।

वैशेषिकाणां कारणद्रव्येषु गन्धाद्यनुमानं तु भाष्येऽस्माभिर्निराकृतम्। अथैवमपि प्रकृतेरणुविभुसाधारणसत्त्वाद्यनेकव्यक्तिरूपत्वेऽपरिच्छिन्नत्वैकत्वाक्रियत्वसिद्धान्तक्षतिरिति मैवम्। कारणद्रव्यत्वरूपप्रकृतित्वेनैवाऽपरिच्छिन्नत्ववचनात्। गन्धत्वेन गन्धानां पृथिवीव्यापकतावत्। आकाशादिप्रकृतीनां विभुत्वेनैव प्रकृतिविभुत्वसिद्धान्तोपपत्तेश्च। तथा पुरुषभेदेन सर्गभेदेन च भेदाभावस्यैवैकशब्दार्थत्वात्। अजामेकामिति श्रुतितस्तथाऽवगमात्। अथाऽध्यवसायाभिमानादिक्रियाराहित्यस्यैवाऽक्रियशब्दार्थत्वात्। अन्यथा श्रुतिस्मृतिपूक्तस्य प्रकृतिक्षोभस्याऽनुपपत्तेरिति। प्रकृतिगताश्चाऽपरे विशेषा भाष्ये द्रष्टव्याः। प्रकृत्यनुमानं चेदम्। सुखदुःखमोहात्मकं महदादिकार्यं सुखदुःखमोहात्मकद्रव्यकार्यं सुखदुःखमोहात्मकत्वात् वस्त्रादिकार्यशय्यादिवदिति। श्रुतिस्मृती चाऽत्राऽनुग्राहकस्तर्कः। एवं सामान्यतोऽनुमितायाः प्रकृतेर्विशेषाः शास्त्राद् योगाच्चाऽवगन्तव्याः। अनुमानस्य सामान्यमात्रविषयकत्वात्। नन्वन्तरेव सुखादिकमुपलभ्यते बाह्यवस्तुषु सुखादौ किं प्रमाणं येन दृष्टान्तता स्यादिति। उच्यते। अन्तःकरणस्य सुखादिहेतुतया विषयेषु सुखादिकं सिध्यति। न च रूपादिगतोत्तमत्वादिकमेव

सुखाद्युत्पादने नियामकम्। उत्तमत्वादेर्जातिरूपत्वे नीलत्वपीतत्वादिना जातिसाङ्कर्यापत्तेः। कालादिभेदैरेकस्या एव रूपव्यक्तेः सुखदुःखोत्पादकत्वाच्च च। अतः सुखादिमत्त्वमेवोत्तमत्वादिकम्। किञ्च घटरूपमिति प्रत्ययवत् स्त्रीसुखं चन्दनसुखमित्यादिप्रत्ययादपि विषये सुखाद्युचितम्। अधिकं तु भाष्ये द्रष्टव्यम्। तदेवं प्रकृतिर्निरूपिता। महत्तत्त्वं निरूप्यते। प्रकृतेः सकाशाद् बुद्ध्याख्यं महत्तत्वं जायते। तस्य धर्मादिरूपप्रकृष्टगुणयोगान् महत्सञ्ज्ञा तदेव च लक्षणम्। महान् बुद्धिः प्रज्ञेत्यादयश्च तस्य पर्यायाः। तथा चोक्तमनुगीतायाम्।

महानात्मा मतिर्विष्णुर्जिष्णुः शम्भुश्च वीर्यवान्।
बुद्धिः प्रज्ञोपलब्धिश्च तथा ब्रह्मा धृतिः स्मृतिः॥
पर्यायवाचकैरेतैर्महानात्मा निगद्यते।
सर्वतः पाणिपादश्च सर्वतोऽक्षिशिरोमुखः॥
सर्वतः श्रुतिमाल्ँ लोके सर्वं व्याप्य स तिष्ठति।
अणिमा लघिमा प्राप्तिरीशानो ज्योतिरव्ययः॥
ज्ञानवन्तश्च ये केचिदलुब्धा जितमन्यवः।
विमुक्ताः सर्व एवैते महत्त्वमुपयान्त्युत॥
विष्णुरेवाऽऽदिसर्गेषु स्वयम्भूर्भवति प्रभुः॥

इति। अत्र सत्त्वाद्यंशत्रयेण महतो देवतात्रयोपाधित्वात् तदविवेकेन ब्रह्मविष्णुशिवत्ववचनम्। तदुक्तं विष्णौ।

सात्त्विको राजसश्चैव तामसश्च त्रिधा महान्।

इति। मात्स्ये च।

सविकारात् प्रधानात् तु महत्तत्त्वमजायत।
महानिति यतः ख्यातिर्लोकानां जायते सदा॥
गुणेभ्यः क्षोभ्यमाणेभ्यस्त्रयो देवा विजज्ञिरे।
एका मूर्तिस्त्रयो देवा ब्रह्मविष्णुमहेश्वराः॥

इति। अणिमेत्यादिभावनिर्देशो धर्माधर्मभेदात्। ब्रह्मशङ्करापेक्षयाऽप्यादौ विष्णुरूपेणैव महानाविर्भवतीति विष्णुरेवेत्यर्थेनोक्तम्। इदमेव महत्तत्त्वमंशतो रजस्तमःसम्भेदेन परिणतं सद् व्यष्टिजीवानामुपाधिरधर्मादियुक्तं क्षुद्रमपि भवति। महदुपरागाद् विपरीतमिति साङ्ख्यसूत्रात्। महत्तत्त्वस्य प्राधान्येनाऽसाधारण्येन चाऽध्यवसायो वृत्तिः। महदहङ्कारमनस्त्रितयात्मकस्यान्तःकरणस्य महत्तत्त्वं बीजावस्थेति। अत्र प्रकृतेर्महान् महतोऽहङ्कार इत्यादिसृष्टिक्रमे शास्त्रमेव प्रमाणम्। अनुमानेन सामान्यतः कार्याणां सकारणकत्वमात्रसिद्धेः न तु सृष्टौ भूतादिक्रमो वाऽन्तःकरणादिक्रमो वेत्येकतरावधारकमनुमानं सम्भवति। स्पष्टलिङ्गाभावात्। श्रुतिस्मृत्यनुगृहीतं यथाकथञ्चित् लिङ्गं तु महदादिक्रमेऽस्तीति भाष्येऽस्माभिः प्रदर्शितम्। महत्तत्त्वं निरूपितम्। अहङ्कारो निरूप्यते। महत्तत्त्वादहङ्कार उत्पद्यते। अङ्कुरात् शाखावत्। तस्य चाऽभिमानवृत्तिकत्वादहङ्कारसञ्ज्ञा। कुम्भकारसञ्ज्ञावत्। तदेव लक्षणम्। तस्य च पर्यायाः कौर्मे प्रोक्ताः।

अहङ्कारोऽभिमानश्च कर्ता मन्ता च संस्मृतः।
आत्मा च प्रकुलो जीवो यतः सर्वाः प्रवृत्तयः॥

इति। स चाऽहङ्कारस्त्रिविधस्तया त्रिविधकार्यहेतुः। तदुक्तं कौमे।

वैकारिकस्तैजसश्च भूतादिश्चैव तामसः।
त्रिविधोऽयमहङ्कारो महतः सम्बभूव ह॥
तैजसादिन्द्रियाणि स्युर्देवा वैकारिकाद् दश।
एकादशं मनश्चाऽत्र स्वगुणेनोभयात्मकम्॥
भूततन्मात्रसर्गस्तु भूतादेरभवन् प्रजाः।

इति। वैकारिकः सात्त्विकः। तैजसो राजसः। स्वगुणेनेन्द्रियवृत्तिषु साधारण्यरूपेणोत्कर्षेण। उभयात्मकं ज्ञानकर्मोभयेन्द्रियात्मकम्। अन्यत्रमना अभूवं नाऽश्रौषमित्यादिश्रुत्या मनसो ज्ञानकर्मोभयेन्द्रियसहकारित्वसिद्धेरिति। एकादशेन्द्रियदेवाश्च।

दिग्वातार्कप्रचेतोऽश्विवह्नीन्द्रोपेन्द्रमित्रकाः।
चन्द्रश्च

इति। अहङ्कारो निरूपितः। इन्द्रियादीनि निरूप्यन्ते। अहङ्कारादादौ मन उत्पद्यते।

शब्दरागाच्छ्रोत्रमस्य जायते भावितात्मनः।
रूपरागात् तथा चक्षुर्घ्राणं गन्धजिघृक्षया॥

इत्यादिना मोक्षधर्मादाविन्द्रियादीनां मनोवृत्तिरागादिकार्यत्वश्रवणात्। ततश्चाऽहङ्कारात् सङ्कल्पपूर्वकं दशेन्द्रियाणि पञ्चतन्मात्राणि चोत्पद्यन्ते। इन्द्रियतन्मात्रयोश्च कार्यकारणभावस्याऽभावात् क्रमनियमो नाऽस्ति। तत्रेन्द्रियेषु ना-

ऽस्त्यवान्तरकार्यकारणभावः प्रमाणाभावात्। तन्मात्रेषु त्वस्ति। स यथा। शब्दतन्मात्राद् वक्ष्यमाणक्रमेण स्पर्शतन्मात्रं शब्दस्पर्शोभयगुणकमेवं क्रमेणैकैकगुणवृद्ध्या परतन्मात्रत्रयं पूर्वपूर्वतन्मात्रेभ्य उत्पद्यते पातञ्जलभाष्ये तन्मात्रेषु क्रमेणैकैकगुणवृद्धिवचनात्। ततश्च पञ्चतन्मात्रेभ्यः पञ्चभूतानि जायन्ते। तत्राऽहङ्कारात् पञ्चतन्मात्राणां तद्द्वारा भूतानां चोत्पत्तौ क्रमः कूर्मविष्णवादिपुराणेषूक्तः। यथा कूर्मे।

भूतादिस्तु विकुर्वाणः शब्दमात्रं ससर्ज ह।
आकाशं सुषिरं तस्मादुत्पन्नं शब्दलक्षणम्॥
आकाशस्तु विकुर्वाणः स्पर्शमात्रं ससर्ज ह।
वायुरुत्पद्यते तस्मात् तस्य स्पर्शो गुणो मतः॥

इत्यादिक्रमेणेति। नन्वेवमाकाशादिभूतचतुष्टयस्याऽपि तत्त्वान्तरारम्भकत्वेन प्रकृतित्वापत्त्या केवलविकृतित्वसिद्धान्तक्षतिरिति चेन् न। आकाशादीनां स्पर्शादितन्मात्रेष्वहङ्कारोपष्टम्भमात्रेण कारणत्वस्य पुराणेषूक्तत्वादिति। तदेवं त्रयोविंशतितत्त्वानामुत्पत्तिरुक्ता। तत्र पञ्चभूतानि वर्जयित्वाऽहङ्कारं च बुद्धौ प्रवेश्य सप्तदशकं लिङ्गशरीरसञ्ज्ञं भवति वह्नेरिन्धनवदात्मनोऽभिव्यक्तिस्थानत्वात्। तच् च सर्वपुरुषाणां सर्गादावुत्पद्य प्राकृतप्रलयपर्यन्तं तिष्ठति। तेनैव चेहलोकपरलोकयोः संसरणं जीवानां भवति। प्राणस्तु बुद्धेरेव वृत्तिभेद इत्यतो न लिङ्गशरीरात् पृथङ् निर्दिश्यते। तस्य लिङ्गशरीरस्य स्वल्पमपि पञ्चभूतान्याश्रयश्चित्रादिवदाश्रयं विना

परमसूक्ष्मस्य लोकान्तरगमनासम्भवात्। इदं च लिङ्गशरीरमादौ स्वयम्भुव उपाधिभूतमेकमेव जायते। तस्यैव विराडाख्यब्रह्माण्डस्थूलशरीरवत्। ततश्च व्यष्टिजीवानामुपाधिभूतानि व्यष्टिलिङ्गशरीराणि तदंशभूतानि ततो विभज्यन्ते। पितुर्लिङ्गशरीरात् पुत्रलिङ्गशरीरवत्। तदुक्तं सूत्रकारेण। व्यक्तिभेदः कर्मविशेषादिति। मनुनाऽप्युक्तम्।

तेषां त्ववयवान् सूक्ष्मान् षण्णामप्यमितौजसाम्।
सन्निवेश्याऽऽत्ममात्रासु सर्वभूतानि निर्ममे॥

इति। षण्णामिति षडिन्द्रियं समस्तलिङ्गशरीरोपलक्षकम्। तथा च स्वयम्भूः स्वलिङ्गशरीरावयवान् सूक्ष्मान् अल्पान् आत्ममात्रासु स्वांशचेतनेषु संयोज्य सर्वप्राणिनः ससर्जेत्यर्थः। लिङ्गशरीरं निरूपितम्। स्थूलशरीरोत्पत्तिरुच्यते। दशगुणितमहत्तत्त्वमध्येऽहङ्कारोऽहङ्कारस्याऽपि दशगुणितस्य मध्ये व्योम व्योम्नोऽपि दशगुणितस्य मध्ये वायुर्वायोरपि दशगुणितस्य मध्ये तेजः तेजसोऽपि दशगुणितस्य मध्ये जलं जलस्याऽपि दशगुणितस्य मध्ये पृथिवी समुत्पद्यते। सैव स्थूलशरीरस्य बीजम्। तदेव च पृथिवीरूपं बीजमण्डरूपेण परिणमते। तस्याऽपि दशगुणितस्याऽण्डरूपस्य पृथिव्यावरणस्य मध्ये चतुर्दशभुवनात्मकं स्वयम्भुवः स्थूलशरीरं तत्सङ्कल्पादेवोत्पद्यते। तेनैव शरीरेण स्वयम्भूर्नारायण इत्युच्यते। तदुक्तं मनुना स्वयम्भुवं प्रकृत्य।

सोऽभिध्याय शरीरात् स्वात् सिसृक्षुर्विविधाः प्रजाः।

अप एव ससर्जाऽऽदौ तासु बीजमवासृजत् ॥
तदण्डमभवद्धैमं सहस्रांशुसमप्रभम् ।
तस्मिं जज्ञे स्वयं ब्रह्मा सर्वलोकपितामहः ॥

स वै शरीरी प्रथमः स वै पुरुष उच्यते ।
आदिकर्ता स भूतानां ब्रह्माऽग्रे समवर्तत ॥

आपो नारा इति प्रोक्ता आपो वै नरसूनवः ।
ता यदस्याऽयनं पूर्वं तेन नारायणः स्मृतः ॥

इत्यादिनेति । तत एव चाऽऽदिपुरुषात् व्यष्टिपुरुषाणां विभागादन्ते च तत्रैव लयात् स एव चैक आत्मेति श्रुतिस्मृत्योर्व्यवह्रियते । अतो न व्यवहारपरतया नारायण एव सर्वभूतानामात्मेति श्रुतिस्मृतिविरोध इति । ततश्च स नारायणो विराट्शरीरी स्वनाभिकमलकर्णिकास्थानीयस्य सुमेरोरुपरि चतुर्मुखाख्यस्वयम्भुवं सृष्ट्वा तद्द्वाराऽन्यानपि व्यष्टिशरीरिणः स्वावरान्तान् ससर्ज । तथा च स्मर्यते ।

तच्छरीरसमुत्पन्नैः कार्यैस्तैः करणैः सह ।
क्षेत्रज्ञाः समजायन्त गात्रेभ्यस्तस्य धीमतः ॥

इति । यत् तु शेषशायिनो नारायणस्य नाभिकमलश्रोत्रचक्षुरादिभ्यश्चतुर्मुखस्याऽऽविर्भावः श्रूयते तद् दैनन्दिनसर्गेष्वेव कल्पभेदेन मन्तव्यम् । दैनन्दिनप्रलयेष्वेव हि नारायणशरीरे प्रविश्यैकीभूय सुप्तानां देवानां चतुर्मुखादिक्रमेणाऽऽविर्भावः शेषशायिनः सकाशाद् घटते न त्वादिसर्गेषु । दैनन्दिनप्रलय

एव लीलाविग्रहेण शयनादिति । तदेवं सङ्क्षेपतश्चतुर्विंशतित-
त्त्वानि तेषां सृष्टिरूपं प्रयोजनं चोक्तम् । तत्र यद् यस्माज् जायते
तस्य तदापूरणेनैव स्थितिः ततस्तस्य संहारोऽपि तत्रैव भवति ।

यद् यस्माज् जायते तत्त्वं तत् तत्र प्रविलीयते ।
लीयन्ते प्रतिलोमानि जायन्ते चोत्तरोत्तरम् ॥

इति भारतादिभ्य इति । एते च सृष्टिस्थितिसंहाररूपाः स्थूला
एव परिणामाश्चतुर्विंशतितत्त्वानां कूटस्थपुरुषविवेकाय प्रद-
र्शिताः । सूक्ष्मा अप्यन्ये प्रतिक्षणपरिणामा एतेषां स्मर्यन्ते । तथा ।

नित्यदा ह्यङ्गभूतानि भवन्ति न भवन्ति च ।
कालेनाऽलक्ष्यवेगेन सूक्ष्मत्वात् तन् न दृश्यते ॥

इति । अतश्च सर्वं जडवस्तु परमार्थतः सर्वदैवाऽसदुच्यते ।
ततश्च तस्माद् विरज्याऽऽत्मैव परमार्थसत्यो दुःखभीरुभिर्द्र-
ष्टव्यः । तदुक्तमनुगीतायाम् ।

अव्यक्तबीजप्रभवो बुद्धिस्कन्धमयो महान् ।
महाहङ्कारविटप इन्द्रियाङ्कुरकोटरः ॥
महाभूतप्रशाखश्च विशेषप्रतिशाखवान् ।
सदापर्णः सदापुष्पः शुभाशुभफलोदयः ॥
आजीवः सर्वभूतानां ब्रह्मवृक्षः सनातनः ।
एतज् ज्ञात्वा च तत्त्वेन ज्ञानेन परमासिना ॥
छित्त्वा चाऽक्षरतां प्राप्य जहाति मृत्युजन्मनी ।

इति श्रीविज्ञानभिक्षुविरचिते साङ्ख्यसारे विवेकप्रतियो-
गिनां प्रकृत्यादीनां स्वरूपपरिच्छेदः ॥ ० ॥

इति साङ्ख्यसारस्य पूर्वभागः ॥

अथोत्तरभागः ॥

प्रथमः परिच्छेदः ॥

अथ शिष्यैः सुखेनैव ग्रहीतुं प्रश्नमालया ।
विवेकस्याऽनुयोगघातमा पुरुषाख्यो निरूप्यते ॥ १ ॥
तत्र सामान्यतः सिद्धो जानेऽहमिति धीबलात् ।
द्रष्टाऽतो नित्यविभ्वादिधर्मैरेव स साध्यते ॥ २ ॥
भोक्ता नित्यस्तदर्थत्वात् तत्कर्मोत्पादितत्वतः ।
महदादिविकाराणां सर्वेषामविशेषतः ॥ ३ ॥
अपि चाऽदृष्टसंस्काराधारत्वाद् बीजरूपतः ।
धीरनादिरतोऽस्यास्य सिद्धा भोक्तुरनादिता ॥ ४ ॥
स्वस्वामिभावानादित्वम्तते भोक्तृव्यवस्थितेः ।
स्वभक्तवृत्तिसंस्कारवत्त्वं स्वत्वं तु बुद्धिषु ॥ ५ ॥
स्वाम्यं स्वनिष्ठसंस्कारहेतुवृत्तेश्च भोक्तरि ।
अतश्च घटते स्वत्वनाशे कैवल्यमात्मनः ॥ ६ ॥
भोक्तुश्चाऽनादिभावस्य विनाशे हेत्वसम्भवात् ।
न नाशो भोक्तुरस्तीति भोक्ता नित्यो हि सिध्यति ॥ ७ ॥
जन्यो ज्ञानप्रकाशोऽस्य नित्यत्वे तु न युज्यते ।
न ह्यप्रकाशे कुत्राऽपि प्रकाशोत्पत्तिरीक्ष्यते ॥ ८ ॥
कार्ये प्रकाशाख्यगुणोऽवयवानां हि तद्गुणः ।
कारणं तेन नाऽनित्यः प्रकाशो नित्यवस्तुनि ॥ ९ ॥

प्रकाशाश्रयसंयोगात् प्रकाशश्चेन्म इन्धने।
आदर्शे चाऽऽवृतेर्भङ्गात् प्रकाशोत्पत्तिविभ्रमः ॥ १० ॥
तस्मान् नित्यात्मनो ज्ञानं नित्यं वाच्यं तथा सति।
लाघवाज् ज्ञानमेवाऽऽत्मा निराधारः प्रकल्प्यते ॥ ११ ॥
अनाश्रिततया द्रव्यं संयोगादेश्च तन् मतम्।
अतो जानेऽहमित्यादिबुद्धिरप्युपपद्यते ॥ १२ ॥
पिण्डेऽहन्धीर्हि मूढानां ध्रुवैवाऽनादिदोषतः।
संयोगात् तत्र पिण्डे तु ज्ञानवत्त्वमतिः प्रमा ॥ १३ ॥
सन्तु वाऽऽधेयताश्यत्वजन्मनाशादिबुद्धयः।
श्रोत्रस्य नभसीवाऽर्थज्ञानस्य ज्ञानमाचके ॥ १४ ॥
तस्माल् लाघवतर्केण बाधकाभावतस्तथा।
श्रुत्यादिभिश्च नित्यात्मा चिद्रूपेणैव सिध्यति ॥ १५ ॥
तज् ज्ञानं विभु नित्यत्वाद् देहव्यापितयाऽपि च।
मध्यत्वे नाशिता हि स्यादणुत्वे वाऽल्पदेशता ॥ १६ ॥
विभुत्वेऽपि स्वधीवृत्तेरेव साक्षान् निरीक्षणात्।
न सर्वत्र सदा सर्वभानं ज्ञाने प्रसज्यते ॥ १७ ॥
अर्थभानं चितावर्थप्रतिबिम्बो मतो बुधैः।
वृत्तेरेव चितौ साक्षात् प्रतिबिम्बनयोग्यता ॥ १८ ॥
अतोऽसङ्गेऽपि कूटस्थचैतन्ये विभुनि ध्रुवे।
वृत्तिद्वारकमेवाऽन्यभानं फलबलान् मतम् ॥ १९ ॥
अन्वयव्यतिरेकाभ्यां वृत्तिजन्यतयाऽखिलः।
वृत्त्यैकाधिकरण्येन कामादिर्धीषु नाऽऽत्मस्तु ॥ २० ॥

अतोऽन्तःस्थविकाराणां स्वस्वबुद्धिष्ववस्थितेः ।
कूटस्थ एव सर्वोऽपि चिदाकाशगणः समः ॥ २१ ॥
नित्यशुद्धो नित्यबुद्धो नित्यमुक्तो निरञ्जनः ।
स्वप्रकाशो निराधारः प्रदीपः सर्ववस्तुषु ॥ २२ ॥
नन्वेवमेकतैवाऽस्तु लाघवादात्मनां खवत् ।
धीष्वेव सुखदुःखादिवैधर्म्यादिति चेन् न तत् ॥ २३ ॥
भोगाभोगादिवैधर्म्यैरेकरूपेऽपि चिद्गणे ।
श्रुतिस्मृतिभ्यामुक्तेन भेदसिद्धेः परस्परम् ॥ २४ ॥
सुखादिप्रतिबिम्बात्मा भोगोऽप्यस्य न वस्तुतः ।
तथाऽप्यस्य चितौ भावाभावौ स्यातां हि भेदकौ ॥ २५ ॥
औपाधिकौ यथा श्यामरागौ स्फटिकभेदकौ ।
खदृष्टान्तस्य विषमो वैधर्म्यासिद्धितोऽम्बरे ॥ २६ ॥

इति श्रीविज्ञानभिक्षुविरचिते साङ्ख्यसारे पुरुषस्वरूपपरिच्छेदः ॥ * ॥

अथ द्वितीयः परिच्छेदः ।

अथाऽऽत्मानात्मवधर्म्यें गुणदोषात्मके तयोः ।
वक्ष्ये विस्तारतो येन विवेकोऽतिस्फुटो भवेत् ॥ १ ॥
सामान्यात्मघनाकाशे सान्निध्येरितशक्तिभिः ।
जायते लीयते भूत्वा भूयोऽयं जगदम्बुदः ॥ २ ॥
त्रिगुणात्मकशक्तीनां परिणामैरतस्थितिः ।
आधारविधया विश्वोपादानमविकारतः ॥ ३ ॥
यथाऽऽधारतया तोयं धरोपादानमिष्यते ।
स्वस्थपार्थिवतन्मात्रद्वारेणैवं चितिर्मता ॥ ४ ॥
अतो जगदुपादानमपि ब्रह्माऽविकारतः ।
कूटस्थनित्यपर्यायपरमार्थसदुच्यते ॥ ५ ॥
स्वार्थत्वात् स्वानुभूत्या च सिद्धत्वात् परमार्थसत् ।
स्वतः स्थित्या स्वतः सिद्ध्या लोकैः सन्निति चीर्यते ॥ ६ ॥
प्रतिक्षणविकारेण तैस्तैः रूपैरपायतः ।
प्रकृत्यादिरसत् सर्वा जडार्थोऽब्धौ तरङ्गवत् ॥ ७ ॥
यत् तु कालान्तरेणाऽपि नाऽन्यसञ्ज्ञामुपैति वै ।
परिणामादिसम्भूतां तद् वस्त्वित्यादिकस्मृतेः ॥ ८ ॥
परार्थाधीनसत्त्वाच् च परदृष्ट्या च सिद्धितः ।
परतः सन्नसन्नेव तत्परापेक्षया मतः ॥ ९ ॥
सतोऽस्तित्वं तु नाऽसत्ता नास्तित्वे सत्यता कुतः ।
इति गारुडतस्त्वैवं सदसत्त्वव्यवस्थितेः ॥ १० ॥

अतो न सन् नाऽसदिदं जगत् सदसदात्मकम् ।
असद्विषयकत्वाच् च तस्य धीस्तात्त्विको भ्रमः ॥ ११ ॥
जगद्वृत्तस्य चैतन्यं सारोऽसारस्तथेतरत् ।
प्रपञ्चस्य स्थिरांशो हि चितिरेवाऽविकारतः ॥ १२ ॥
तदन्यदखिलं तुच्छमसारत्वादुदीर्यते ।
तथाऽनृतमसच् चाऽपि तदपेक्षास्थिरत्वतः ॥ १३ ॥
एवंविधैवाऽऽत्मसत्ता अन्यासत्ता च दर्शिता ।
वासिष्ठादौ विस्तरतो यथा लेशात् तदुच्यते ॥ १४ ॥
स्वप्नो जाग्रत्यसद्रूपः स्वप्ने जाग्रदसद्वपुः ॥
मृतिर्जन्मन्यसद्रूपा मृतौ जन्माऽप्यसन्मयम् ॥ १५ ॥
जगन्मयी भ्रान्तिरिति न कदाऽपि न विद्यते ।
विद्यते न कदाचिच् च जलबुद्बुदवत् स्थितम् ॥ १६ ॥
आत्मैवाऽस्ति परं सत्यं नाऽन्याः संसारदृष्टयः ।
शुक्तिकारजतं यद्वद् यथा मरुमरीचिका ॥ १७ ॥
अस्ति सर्वगतं शान्तं परमात्मघनं शुचि ।
अचिन्त्यचिन्मात्रवपुः परमाकाशमाततम् ॥ १८ ॥
तत् सर्वगं सर्वशक्ति सर्वं सर्वात्मकं स्वयम् ।
यत्र यत्र यथोदेति तथाऽऽस्ते तत्र तत्र वै ॥ १९ ॥
आविर्भावतिरोभावमयास्त्रिभुवनोर्मयः ।
स्फुरन्त्यतितते यस्मिन् मराविव मरीचयः ॥ २० ॥
असतेव सती तोयनद्येव लहरी चला ।
मनसैवेन्द्रजालश्रीर्जागती प्रवितन्यते ॥ २१ ॥

ब्रह्मणा तन्यते विश्वं मनसैव स्वयम्भुवा।
मनोमयमतो विश्वं यन् नाम परिदृश्यते॥ २२॥
यो ह्यप्रबुद्धमतिर्मूढो रूढो न वितते पदे।
वज्रसारमिदं तस्य जगदस्त्यसदेव सत्॥ २३॥
अव्युत्पन्नस्य कनके कानके कटके यथा।
कटकज्ञप्तिरेवाऽस्ति न मनागपि हेमधीः॥ २४॥
तथाऽज्ञस्य पुरागारनगनागेन्द्रभासुरा।
इयं दृश्यदृगेवाऽस्ति न त्वन्या परमार्थदृक्॥ २५॥
इत्यादिवाक्यैर्वासिष्ठे नाऽत्यन्तासत्यतोदिता।
जगतोऽपरवाक्यैर्हि सत् कार्यं प्राकृतं मतम्॥ २६॥
नामरूपविनिर्मुक्तं यस्मिन् सन्तिष्ठते जगत्।
तमाहुः प्रकृतिं केचिन् मायामेकेऽपरे त्वणून्॥ २७॥
सुषुप्तावस्थया चक्रपद्मरेखा शिलोदरे।
यथा स्थिता चितेरन्तस्तथेयं जगदावली॥ २८॥
प्रकृतिव्रततिर्व्योम्नि जाता ब्रह्माण्डसत्फला।
इत्यादिवाक्यैः साङ्ख्यीयसत्कार्याद्युपवर्णनात्॥ २९॥

इति श्रीविज्ञानभिक्षुविरचिते साङ्ख्यसारे आत्मानात्मनोः सत्यत्वासत्यत्ववैधर्म्यपरिच्छेदः॥ * ॥

अथ तृतीयः परिच्छेदः ॥

तदेवमात्मनः सत्ता दर्शिताऽन्यविलक्षणा ।
अथ चिद्रूपतां वक्ष्ये बुद्धिवृत्तिविलक्षणाम् ॥ १ ॥
अनुभूतिस्थितिर्बोधो वेदनं चोच्यते पुमान् ।
वेद्यं जडं तमोऽज्ञानं प्रधानादिकमुच्यते ॥ २ ॥
वेदनं वेद्यसम्बन्धादेव वेत्त्रभिधीयते ।
यथा प्रकाश्यसम्बन्धात् प्रकाशोऽपि प्रकाशकः ॥ ३ ॥
यथा वाऽर्थोपरागेण भानमर्थस्य भासकम् ।
एवं वेद्योपरक्तस्याऽस्वांशस्याऽऽधारताऽऽत्मनि ॥ ४ ॥
असङ्गायां चितौ वेद्योपरागोऽयं न धीष्विव ।
किन्तु साक्षाद् द्वारतो वा चिति तत्प्रतिबिम्बनम् ॥ ५ ॥
बाह्यं वृत्त्याख्यकरणाभावादनुपरागतः ।
चितिर्नैवेक्षते चेत्यं विभुत्वेऽपि च सर्वतः ॥ ६ ॥
तथा चिदपि वृत्त्याख्यकरणाभावतोऽर्थवत् ।
स्वगोचरां वृत्तिमृते तिष्ठत्यज्ञातसत्तया ॥ ७ ॥
तदेवं चिन् निराकारा प्रकाशाकाशरूपिणी ।
तिष्ठत्यव्यक्तरूपा च मोक्षादौ वृत्त्यभावतः ॥ ८ ॥
बुद्धिवृत्तिस्तु साकारा परिच्छिन्ना च दीपवत् ।
व्यक्ता च सर्वदा तद्वदसङ्ख्या क्षणभङ्गुरा ॥ ९ ॥
जडा च परदृश्यत्वाद् घटदीपादिवन् मता ।
वृत्तेः प्रकाशता त्वर्थाकारत्वादक्षतैव हि ॥ १० ॥
यथाऽऽस्याकारताहेत्वादादर्शस्तत्प्रकाशकः ।
सर्वाकारत्वयोग्यत्वात् सैवं सर्वप्रकाशिका ॥ ११ ॥

न पुनर्वृत्तिद्रष्टृत्वं चितस्तद्भिन्नद्रष्टृता।
वृत्तेर्यतो गौरवं स्याद् द्वयोर्ज्ञातृत्वकल्पने ॥ १२ ॥
बुद्ध्यारूढं त्वन्यवस्तु तद्द्वारा प्रतिबिम्बितम्।
पश्यत्यनुभवो नाऽन्यो द्रष्टा बुद्ध्यादिकोऽखिलः ॥ १३ ॥
इत्येवं बुद्धिवृत्तिभ्यो वैलक्षण्यं चितीरितम्।
चिदचित्त्वाख्यवैधर्म्यं देहादिभ्यः स्फुटन्त्विदम् ॥ १४ ॥
अन्योन्यप्रतिबिम्बेन सारूप्याद् वृत्तिबोधयोः।
बोधव्यवहृतिर्वृत्तौ लोहेऽग्निव्यवहारवत् ॥ १५ ॥
नैवाऽल्पबुद्ध्याशक्योऽयं विवेको वृत्तिबोधयोः।
तार्किका यत्र सम्मूढाः साङ्ख्याना श्रेष्ठता यतः ॥ १६ ॥
विज्ञानवादिनो बौद्धा वृत्तिबोधाविवेकतः।
ज्ञातात्मत्वश्रुतौ मूढा मेनिरे क्षणिकां चितिम् ॥ १७ ॥
सत्त्वपुंसो विवेकोऽयं वृत्तितद्बोधरूपयोः।
नाऽशक्यः सुधियां यद्वद्धंसानां क्षीरनीरयोः ॥ १८ ॥
एतदन्तश्च संसारो मोक्षस्तत्रैव संस्थितः।
यद् वृत्तिभ्यो विवेकेन तद्बोधस्याऽवधारणम् ॥ १९ ॥
सर्वोऽप्यनुभवं वेद न कश्चिदपि वेदताम्।
विवेकमात्रमस्मिन् हि भासमानेऽप्यपेक्षते ॥ २० ॥
आत्मा विवेक्तुं बाह्यार्थैं न शक्यो वृत्तिमिश्रणात्।
अतो वृत्तौ विवेक्तव्यो वृत्तिबोधतयैव सः ॥ २१ ॥
यथा बुद्ध्या विवेकार्हो नाऽग्निरङ्गारमिश्रणात्।
सोऽङ्गारे तु विवेकार्हो काष्ठदग्धृतया स्फुटम् ॥ २२ ॥

अतएव श्रुतौ स्वप्ने दृश्यवृत्तिविवेकतः ।
स्वयंज्योतिःस्वरूपेण तस्या द्रष्टा प्रदर्शितः ॥ २३ ॥
साक्षात् प्रकाशो यो यस्य स तद्भिन्नो मतो बुधैः ।
घटादिभ्यो यथाऽऽलोक आलोकाच्च चाऽपि वृत्तयः॥२४॥
वृत्तेः साक्षात् प्रकाशत्वादतो ऽनुभवरूपकः ।
वृत्तिभ्यो भिन्न आत्मेति शीघ्रो मार्गः स्वदर्शने ॥ २५ ॥
एवमादिप्रकारेण बुद्धिसत्त्वप्रकाशतः ।
विलक्षणतया सिद्धश्चित्प्रकाशोऽस्य भासकः ॥ २६ ॥
स्वप्नदेहादिदृष्टान्तैस्तस्माच्छ्रुत्यादिदर्शितैः ।
जाग्रद्देहेन्द्रियार्थेभ्यश्चितिर्भिन्नतया मता ॥ २७ ॥
स्वप्ने देहादिकं सर्वं चिद्भिन्नं चिति भासते ।
जाग्रत्येवं विशेषस्तु यद् बाह्यमपि भासते ॥ २८ ॥
स्वप्ने मनोमयत्वाच्च साक्षाच्चिद्विषयोऽखिलम् ।
करणद्वारतो बाह्यं चितो जाग्रति गोचरः ॥ २९ ॥
सर्वं देहादिकं स्वप्नजाग्रतोरेकरूपतः ।
भाति चिद्व्योम्नि नाऽन्त्यार्थबाह्यान्तर्भेदतो भिदा ॥ ३० ॥
चिद्व्योम्नि वासनातो धीः प्रमाणाद् वाऽर्थरूपिणी।
ततश्चितोऽर्थभानं यत् तत् समं स्वप्नजाग्रतोः ॥ ३१ ॥
तदिदं स्वानुभूत्यैव प्रोच्यते न परोक्षतः ।
स्वप्नदृष्टान्तसदृशो नोपायोऽस्त्याऽऽत्मदर्शने ॥ ३२ ॥
सुषुप्तौ हि यथा स्वप्ने स्वात्मन्येवेक्षतेऽखिलम् ।
आत्मानं चैकदेशस्थं मन्यते जागरे तथा ॥ ३३ ॥

सुषुप्तिरात्मनस्तत्त्वं स्वरूपावस्थितेस्तदा।
जाग्रत्स्वप्नौ मायिकौ तु मृषासारूप्यतो धिया॥ ३४॥
बुद्धेः सुषुप्तिस्तमसाऽऽवरणं तद्विलक्षणा।
चितेः सुषुप्तिर्वृत्त्याख्यदृश्यावरणशून्यता॥ ३५॥
पूर्णः कूटस्थनित्यश्च स्वस्वधीमात्रवृत्तिदृक्।
वृत्त्याख्यदृश्यविरहात् सर्वदा नेक्षते पुमान्॥ ३६॥
वृत्तिदेशे यथा बोधस्तथा सर्वत्र सर्वदा।
वृथैव तप्यते मूढैर्व्ययनाशादिनाऽऽत्मनः॥ ३७॥
दुःखभोगमहारोगनिदानं देहगेहिनी।
बुद्धिर्न त्यज्यते मूढैर्महानिद्रासुखं यतः॥ ३८॥
अनादिबुद्धिगार्हस्थ्यं विवेकस्त्यज्यते न चेत्।
न मोक्षो बाह्यसन्न्यासादिहाऽमुत्राऽसुखं परम्॥ ३९॥
समचिन्मात्ररूपेषु स्वपरात्मसु सर्वदा।
बुद्धिमात्रविवेकेन स्वपरादिभिदा मृषा॥ ४०॥
चिन्मात्रे निर्गुणे स्वामिन्यारोप्यैवाऽऽत्मकर्तृताम्।
स्वाम्यवज्ञापराधेन बध्यते धीः स्वकर्मभिः॥ ४१॥
साध्वी तु धीः पतिं दृष्ट्वा याथातथ्येन तत्परा।
इहाऽऽनन्दमयी चाऽन्ते पतिदेहे लयं व्रजेत्॥ ४२॥
नाहं कर्ता सुखी दुःखी चिन्मात्राकाशरूपकः।
एवं नाथं चिन्तयन्ती न पत्युर्दुःखभोगदा॥ ४३॥

इति श्रीविज्ञानभिक्षुविरचिते साङ्ख्यसारे आत्मानात्मनोश्चिदचित्त्ववैधर्म्यपरिच्छेदः॥ ० ॥

अथ चतुर्थः परिच्छेदः ॥

इत्यवमात्मनः प्रोक्तो बुद्ध्यादिभ्यो विलक्षणः ।
चित्प्रकाशोऽधुनाऽऽनन्दरूपता वक्ष्यते तथा ॥ १ ॥
दुःखं कामसुखापेक्षा सुखं दुःखसुखात्ययः ।
इति स्मृतेः सुखात्मत्वं नित्यनिर्दुःखताऽऽत्मनः ॥ २ ॥
परिभाषाबलाद् रूढिबाधः सर्वत्र सम्मतः ।
अन्यथा परिभाषेयं मोक्षशास्त्रे भवेद् वृथा ॥ ३ ॥
यद्वा परोक्षवादेन परमप्रियताप्तये ।
रूपिका सुखगीः पुंसि विभुत्वाप्त्यै खमन्दवत् ॥ ४ ॥
नाऽऽनन्दं न निरानन्दमित्यादिश्रुतिभिः स्फुटम् ।
आत्मन्यानन्दरूपत्वनिषेधाद् युक्तिसंयुतात् ॥ ५ ॥
उपास्याद्यर्थशून्यत्वान् नेति नेति श्रुतेस्तथा ।
निषेधवाक्यं बलवद् विधिवाक्यादिति स्थितिः ॥ ६ ॥
निर्निरानन्दमिति च स्वोपाध्यानन्दभोक्तृताम् ।
स्वामित्वरूपिणीं वक्ति न निर्धन इतीव हि ॥ ७ ॥
प्रेयोऽन्यस्माच्च सर्वस्मादिति श्रुत्या सुखादपि ।
उक्त आत्मा प्रियस्तस्य सुखत्वोक्तिश्च नोचिता ॥ ८ ॥
आनन्दाद्याः प्रधानस्य इति वेदान्तसूत्रतः ।
वेदान्तेऽपि न सिद्धान्त आत्मनः सुखरूपता ॥ ९ ॥
विस्तराद् ब्रह्ममीमांसाभाष्येऽस्माभिः परीक्षितम् ।
चितेरसुखरूपत्वं प्रेमा व्याख्यायतेऽधुना ॥ १० ॥

मा न भूवमहं शश्वद् भूयासमितिरूपकः ।
निर्निमित्तोऽनुरागो यः स प्रेमा परमस्थिति ॥ ११ ॥
अन्याशेषतया बुद्धेः स्नेहोऽयं न सुखेष्वपि ।
अतः प्रियतमः स्वात्मा नाऽन्योऽतो ह्यधिकः प्रियः ॥ १२ ॥
आत्मत्वेनाऽऽत्मनि प्रेमा न सुखत्वाद्यपेक्षते ।
अहं स्यामिति चेद् यस्मात् सुखं स्यामिति नेष्यते ॥ १३ ॥
तथा च सुखतादुःखाभावते वाऽऽत्मताऽपि च ।
प्रेम्णि प्रयोजिका सिद्धा स्वतःप्रेमात्मतैव तु ॥ १४ ॥
तस्माद् वस्तुत आत्मैव प्रियो नौपाधिकत्वतः ।
औपाधिकीतरप्रीतिरस्थिरत्वान् न तात्त्विकी ॥ १५ ॥
प्रीतिरन्यत्र चाऽनित्याऽविवेकाद्यैः सुखादिषु ।
आत्मप्रीतिस्तु नित्याऽतोनित्यानन्दः पुमान् मतः ॥ १६ ॥
आत्मनः प्रियतां बुद्धिर्यदि पश्येत् समाहिता ।
सर्वातिशायिनीं तर्हि सुखाब्धौ किं न मज्जति ॥ १७ ॥
प्रियदर्शनतो बुद्धेः सुखं लोकेषु दृश्यते ।
अतोऽनुमेयं परमप्रियदृष्ट्या परं सुखम् ॥ १८ ॥
आत्मार्थत्वेन सर्वत्र प्रीतिरात्मा स्वतः प्रियः ।
इति शश्वच्छ्रुतिः प्राह आत्मदृष्टिविधित्सया ॥ १९ ॥
ततोऽप्यनुपमं ज्ञेयं प्रियात्मेक्षणतः सुखम् ।
भुञ्जते तत् सुखं धीरा जीवन्मुक्ता महाधियः ॥ २० ॥
अन्तरात्मसुखं सत्यमविसंवादि योगिनम् ।
अपश्यन् कृपणो बाह्यसुखार्थी वञ्चितो जनः ॥ २१ ॥

सुखाशया बहिः पश्यन् देही चेन्द्रियरन्ध्रकैः ।
वातायनैर्गृहीत्वाऽन्तः सुखं वेत्ति न बाह्यदृक् ॥ २२ ॥

दुःखलभ्यान् दुःखमयान् परिणामेऽतिदुःखदान् ।
विषयोत्थान् सुखाभासान् धिक् स्वात्मसुखरोधकान् ॥२३॥

इति श्रीविज्ञानभिक्षुविरचिते साङ्ख्यसारे आत्मानात्मनोः प्रियाप्रियत्ववैधर्म्यपरिच्छेदः ॥ * ॥

अथ पञ्चमः परिच्छेदः ।

परिच्छेदत्रयेणोक्तं सच्चिदानन्दरूपकम् ।
गीयमानं श्रुतिस्मृत्योरात्मनो लक्षणत्रयम् ॥ १ ॥

तद्वैपरीत्यमन्येषां लक्षणं चेरितं स्फुटम् ।
आभ्यां तु गुणदोषाभ्यां विवेको दोषवत् परः ॥ २ ॥

नैर्गुण्यसगुणत्वादिवैधर्म्याण्यपराण्यपि ।
बहूनि वक्ष्ये सङ्क्षेपात् पुम्प्रकृत्योरतः परम् ॥ ३ ॥

धियोऽर्थाकारया वृत्त्या जनितत्वात् सुखादयः ।
सामानाधिकरण्येन कल्प्यन्ते लाघवाद् धियाम् ॥ ४ ॥

महदादेर्जडत्वेन तद्धेतुश्च जडो मतः ।
कार्यकारणसाजात्यं दृष्टं लोके हि सर्वतः ॥ ५ ॥

अत आत्मा बोधमात्रतया सिध्यति लाघवात् ।
गुणाः सर्वे प्रकृत्यादेर्विकारास्तेतरेऽखिलाः ॥ ६ ॥

आत्मा तु निर्गुणस्तद्वत् कूटस्थश्च मतो बुधैः ।
चितेः कूटस्थसञ्ज्ञा तु स्थिरत्वाद् गिरिकूटवत् ॥ ७ ॥

लेपश्चेतरसम्बन्धे तद्रूपैरुपरक्तता।
यथा विषयसम्बन्धाद् बुद्धौ भवति वासना ॥ ८ ॥
भाण्डादौ द्रव्ययोगाच्च च तत्तद्द्रव्यस्य वासना।
लेपहेतुश्च सम्बन्धः सङ्गः सम्बन्धि चाऽञ्जनम् ॥ ९ ॥
अतो निरञ्जनोऽसङ्गो निर्लेपश्चोच्यते पुमान्।
नभःपुष्करपत्रादिदृष्टान्तैः परमर्षिभिः ॥ १० ॥
चिन्मात्रानन्तशक्त्यब्धौ पुमर्थपवनेरिताः।
सत्त्वादिशक्तयो यान्ति विश्वबुद्बुदरूपताम् ॥ ११ ॥
अत ईशश्चिदात्मैव जगतः सन्निधानतः।
मणिवत् प्रेरकत्वेन जडानामयसामिव ॥ १२ ॥
पुमानेव जगत्कर्ता जगद्भर्ताऽखिलेश्वरः।
स्वाम्यर्थे भृत्यवद् यस्माज् जडवर्गः प्रवर्तते ॥ १३ ॥
करणानि च देहेषु राजार्थमधिकारिवत्।
भोग्यजातं मनोमन्त्रिण्यर्पयन्ति स्वभावतः ॥ १४ ॥
तैर्भोग्यैर्युक्तमात्मानमावेदयति धीश्चिति।
इच्छामात्रेण तद् भुङ्क्ते राजेवाऽऽत्माऽखिलेश्वरः ॥ १५ ॥
धनादेरीश्वरो देहो देहस्येन्द्रियमीश्वरम्।
इन्द्रियस्येश्वरी बुद्धिर्बुद्धेरात्मेश्वरः परः ॥ १६ ॥
कूटस्थस्येश्वरस्याऽन्यो नाऽस्ति प्रेरक इत्यतः।
ईश्वरस्याऽवधित्वेन द्रष्टा वै परमेश्वरः ॥ १७ ॥
अन्यस्याऽऽगन्तुकैश्वर्यं बहुव्यापारसङ्कुलम्।
निर्व्यापारस्य निर्दोषमनाद्यैश्वर्यमात्मनः ॥ १८ ॥

सर्वशक्तिमयो ह्यात्मा शक्तिमण्डलताण्डवः ।
संसारं तन्निवृत्तिं च माययाऽऽप्नोति हेलया ॥ १९ ॥
सर्वातिशायि निर्दोषमैश्वर्यमिदमात्मनः ।
पश्यतो योगिनो ब्राह्ममप्यैश्वर्यं तृणायते ॥ २० ॥
बाह्यस्याऽऽत्मोच्यते देहो देहस्याऽऽत्मेन्द्रियाणि च ।
बुद्धिरात्मेन्द्रियाणां तस्य बुद्धेरात्मा तु चिन्नभः ॥ २१ ॥
अत आत्मावधित्वेन परमात्मोच्यते चितिः ।
तथाऽन्तःकरणैर्योगाज् जीव इत्युच्यते चितिः ॥ २२ ॥
अविद्याकार्यरहितः परमात्मेति च स्मृतिः ।
यस्य यद् व्यापकं तस्य तद् ब्रह्माऽतो धरादिकम् ॥२३॥
प्रकृत्यन्तं भवेद् ब्रह्म स्वस्वकार्याद्यपेक्षया ।
सेश्वरे साङ्ख्यवादेऽपि चितेरेवाऽनुमन्यते ॥ २४ ॥
परे वा परमात्मत्वादिकं तु न जडे क्वचित् ।
अध्यक्षव्यापकत्वाभ्यां परं ब्रह्म तु चेतनः ॥ २५ ॥
तस्याऽध्यक्षं व्यापकं च न हेतुविधयाऽस्ति हि ।
असङ्गात्मा नभोराशिरविभक्तैकरूपकः ॥ २६ ॥
सोऽतस्चिद्घनविज्ञानघनात्मघनसंज्ञकः ।
प्रकाशस्याऽनपेक्षत्वात् स्वस्य द्रष्टृतयाऽपि च ॥ २७ ॥
स्वप्रकाशः पुमानुक्त इतरे तद्विलक्षणाः ।
भोगोऽभ्यवहृतिः सा च कूटस्थे नाऽस्ति धीष्विव ॥ २८ ॥
धीवृत्तिप्रतिबिम्बाख्यगौणभोगा तु भोक्तृता ।
साक्षाद् धीवृत्तिद्रष्टृत्वाद् बुद्धिसाक्ष्युच्यते पुमान् ॥ २९ ॥

विना विकारं द्रष्टृत्वात् साक्षी ह्युक्तोऽखिलस्य सः।
चैत्योपरागरूपत्वात् साक्षिताऽप्यध्रुवा चितः॥ ३०॥
उपलक्षणमेवेदमपि व्यावृत्तये जडात्।
अतः पुमाननिर्देश्योऽणुश्च सूक्ष्मश्च कथ्यते॥ ३१॥
विना दृश्यमदृश्यत्वादव्यक्तश्चोच्यते सतः।
अदृश्यो दृश्यते राऊर्गृहीतेन यथेन्दुना॥ ३२॥
अदृश्यं चाऽस्यमादर्शे चित् तथा स्वबुद्धिषु।
चिति विश्वस्य सङ्क्षेप् विश्वं भासेत सर्वदा॥ ३३॥
विश्वाधारोऽप्यतः शून्यमिति चिद्गीयते खवत्।
दृश्यदोषान् मृषाबुद्धिर्दृष्टयाऽऽरोप्य निर्मले॥ ३४॥
आदर्शे मलवद् व्योम्नि दोषदृष्ट्या तु तप्यते।
वस्तुतस्त्विति नाऽस्त्येव मलो दृश्याश्रितः सदा॥ ३५॥
अतश्च निर्मलः स्वस्थो निर्दोषश्चोच्यते पुमान्।
सजातीयेषु वैधर्म्यलक्षणा नाऽस्ति यद् भिदा॥ ३६॥
अत आत्मा समः प्रोक्त एकरूप्याच्च सर्वदा।
देहाध्यक्षतया देही पुर्यभिव्यक्तितः पुमान्॥ ३७॥
एकाकित्वादद्वितीयः केवलश्चोच्यते तु सः।
चिच्छन्नप्रतिबन्धेन प्रोच्यतेऽनावृतः पुमान्॥ ३८॥
सर्वस्वामितया चाऽऽत्मा क्षेत्रज्ञः क्षेत्रवेदनात्।
हृत्सरोवरधीपद्मदलवृत्तिषु लीलया॥ ३९॥
चरन्निवाऽऽनन्दमीनान् भुञ्जानो हंस उच्यते।
हकारेण बहिर्याति सकारेण विशन् पुनः॥ ४०॥

प्राणवृत्त्याऽनय चाऽपि प्राणयत्मा हंस उच्यते ।
शरीरागारिहृद्धामगुहायां बुद्धिभार्यया ॥ ४१ ॥
व्यज्यमानस्तया सार्धं स्वपन्निव गुहाशयः ।
त्रिगुणात्मकमायां स्वां सान्निध्यात् परिणामयन् ॥ ४२ ॥
मायोति कथ्यते चाऽऽत्मा तत्कृतान्तवेषधृक् ।
खान्येकादश भूतानि पञ्चैतानि तु षोडश ॥ ४३ ॥
पुंसः कलास्तत्त्वतस्तु निरंशत्वात् स निष्कलः ।
अहंशब्दः स्वामिवाचो स्वामो साक्षी तु चेतसः ॥ ४४ ॥
अतोऽहमिति शब्देन चिन्मात्रं प्रोच्यते बुधैः ।
सर्वेश्वरः सर्ववेत्ता सर्वकर्ताऽद्वयः पुमान् ॥ ४५ ॥
सामान्यादुच्यते यद्वद् राजा सर्वनराधिपः ।
आत्माद्वैतस्य सूत्रेण जातिमात्रेण वर्णनात् ॥ ४६ ॥
प्रलये हि विजातीयद्वैतशून्यत्वमात्मनाम् ।
असङ्गत्वान् नित्यशुद्धो नित्यबुद्धश्च चित्त्वतः ॥ ४७ ॥
नित्यमुक्तस्तथा नित्यनिर्दुःखत्वात् पुमान् मतः ।
इत्यादिगुरुशास्त्रोक्तदिशा स्वानुभवेन च ॥ ४८ ॥
वैधर्म्यादात्मनोऽनात्मविवेकः क्रियतां बुधैः ।
परिच्छेदचतुष्केण पुम्प्रकृत्योः सुविस्तरात् ।
वैधर्म्यगण उक्तोऽयं ध्यायिनामाशु मुक्तिदः ॥ ४९ ॥

इति श्रीविज्ञानभिक्षुविरचिते साङ्ख्यसारे आत्मवैधर्म्यगणपरिच्छेदः ॥ * ॥

अथ षष्ठः परिच्छेदः ।

विवेकमेव सद्युक्त्या मत्वा तदनुभूयते ।
राजयोगं यथा कुर्यात् समासेन तदुच्यते ॥ १ ॥
अशक्तो राजयोगस्य हठयोगेऽधिकारवान् ।
वासिष्ठे हि वसिष्ठाय भुसुण्डेनैवमीरितम् ॥ २ ॥
ज्ञानावृत्ती राजयोगे प्राणायामासने हठे ।
मुख्ये तेऽङ्गतयाऽन्योन्यं सेव्ये शक्त्यनुसारतः ॥ ३ ॥
विषयेऽनन्तदोषा ये श्रुतिस्मृतिसमीरिताः ।
त आदौ परिद्रष्टव्याश्चित्तस्थैर्याय योगिभिः ॥ ४ ॥
कामबीजान्यनन्तानि सम्प्ररोहन्ति यद्धृदि ।
तस्याऽटवीनिभे ज्ञानपुण्यसस्यं न वर्धते ॥ ५ ॥
दोषदृष्ट्यग्निसन्दग्धे कामबीजे तु चेतसि ।
गुरुशास्त्रजलैः सृष्टे सुक्षेत्रे तद्विवर्धते ॥ ६ ॥
सत्येष्वसत्तां प्रचुरां तथा रम्येष्वरम्यताम् ।
सुखेषु प्रचुरं दुःखं पश्यन् धीरो विरज्यते ॥ ७ ॥
ब्रह्मलोकोऽपि नरको विनाशामेध्यपूरितः ।
युक्तश्च स्वाधिकैरन्यैस्त्रैगुण्यादपि दुःखयुक् ॥ ८ ॥
तत्रत्यैरपि मुक्त्यर्थं यत्यते जन्मभीरुभिः ।
अतो ज्ञेयः समासेन लोकः सर्वोऽपि दुःखयुक् ॥ ९ ॥
इदं मे स्यादिदं मा स्यादितीच्छाव्यथितं मनः ।
स्वभावात् तेन विज्ञेयं दुःखं चित्तेन सङ्गतिः ॥ १० ॥

सुखं सुषुप्तिः परमा दुःखं विषयवेदनम् ।
सुखदुःखसमासोऽयं किमन्यैर्बहुभाषितैः ॥ ११ ॥
तस्मादनर्थानर्थाभान् परीक्ष्य विषयान् सुधीः ।
उत्सृजेत् परमार्थार्थी बालरम्यानक्षीनिव ॥ १२ ॥
इत्यादिकानन्तदोषदृष्ट्या रागस्य तानवे ।
मायाविवेकतः शुद्धमात्मानं चिन्तयेत् सदा ॥ १३ ॥
इदं तदिति निर्देष्टुं गुरुणाऽपि न शक्यते ।
उदासीनस्याऽऽत्मतत्त्वं स्वयमेव प्रकाशते ॥ १४ ॥
बुद्धिबोधात्मको बुद्धिसाक्षी बुद्धेः परो विभुः ।
कूटस्थोऽहं चिदादित्य इत्येकाग्रोऽनुचिन्तयेत् ॥ १५ ॥
वृत्तिबोधो घटच्छिद्रमिव नाप्यस्य इष्यते ।
वस्तुतो वृत्तिबोधोऽहं पूर्णो व्योमवदक्षयः ॥ १६ ॥
अन्तर्यद् दृश्यते सर्वं तद् बुद्धेर्वृत्तिरुच्यते ।
तेभ्यो दुःखात्मकेभ्योऽहं साक्षात् तद्वीक्षिता पृथक् ॥ १७ ॥
कर्मकर्तृविरोधो हि वृत्त्या वृत्तिप्रकाशने ।
वृत्तिधाराकल्पने च गौरवादिति निश्चितम् ॥ १८ ॥
हर्षशोकभयक्रोधलोभमोहमदैस्तथा ।
द्वेषाभिमानकार्पण्यनिद्रालस्यस्मरादिभिः ॥ १९ ॥
धर्माधर्मैश्च सम्पूर्णा बुद्धिर्दुःखमयी तु मे ।
आत्मानं दर्शयत्येव भास्करायेव रोगिणः ॥ २० ॥
अहं सर्वगतं शान्तं परमात्मघनं शुचि ।
अचिन्त्यचिन्मात्रनभो विश्वदर्पणमक्षयम् ॥ २१ ॥

निरञ्जनं निराधारं निर्गुणं निरुपद्रवम्।
निर्विशेषं सजातीयात् समस्तार्थावभासकम् ॥ २२ ॥
ब्रह्मविष्णुमहेशाद्याः स्थावरान्ताश्च चेतनाः।
अवैधर्म्यात्मकाभेदादहमित्यनुचिन्तयेत् ॥ २३ ॥
अहमन्ये च पुरुषाः समचिद्व्योमरूपिणः।
अत आत्मैक एवाऽहमिति श्रुतिषु गीयते ॥ २४ ॥
इति पश्यन् स्वभोगैश्च योगी विश्वं प्रपूजयेत्।
आत्मयागोऽप्ययं प्रोक्तः श्रुत्युक्तः साङ्ख्ययोगिनाम्॥२५॥
सर्वभूतस्थमात्मानं सर्वभूतानि चाऽऽत्मनि।
समं पश्यन्नात्मयाजी स्वाराज्यमधिगच्छति ॥ २६ ॥
इत्येवं मनुनाऽप्यात्मयागो ज्ञानाङ्गमीरितः।
तस्मादभयदानेन स्वभोगाद्यर्चनेन च ॥ २७ ॥
सम्मानयन् भूतजातमात्मानमनुचिन्तयेत्।
ब्रह्मविष्णुशिवादीनां भोगे रागश्च हीयते ॥ २८ ॥
तेषां स्वसाम्यदृष्ट्याऽतः साम्यं योगी विचिन्तयेत्।
उत्पत्तौ प्रलये चैव सर्वावस्थासु सर्वदा ॥ २९ ॥
सर्वेषामेकरूपत्व द्रष्टूरागादिकं कुतः।
विष्णवादयो महैश्वर्यं भुञ्ज ना अपि नाऽधिकाः ॥ ३० ॥
मत्तोऽतोऽलं तदैश्वर्यैरविवेकिजनप्रियैः।
गुणकर्मादिभिः किञ्चिन् निरीच्याऽधिकमात्मनः ॥३१॥
तदर्थं यतते लोको नाऽहं पश्यामि मेऽधिकम्।
तथा न्यूनं न पश्यामि यदतिक्रमशङ्कया ॥ ३२ ॥

देवा दैत्यजयायेव यतिष्ये तज्जयाशया ।
अहं यथा तथैवाऽन्ये आब्रह्मा नारका जनाः ॥ ३३ ॥
दृश्यन्ते स्वात्मवत् प्रेम्णा पितृभ्रातृसुतादिवत् ।
क ईश ईशितव्यो वा कः श्रेष्ठः कोऽधमोऽपि वा ॥ ३४ ॥
अभिन्ने भेददृष्ट्या स्यान् मृत्योर्भयमिति श्रुतिः ।
चिद्व्योमस्वेकरूपेषु ईशानीशादिरूपकः ॥ ३५ ॥
रूपभेदो ह्यसन् सर्वः स्फटिके रूपभेदवत् ।
धियां रूपैः पुमानेको बहुरूप इवेयते ॥ ३६ ॥
वृकचर्मादिरूपाद्यैर्मायीव बहुरूपधृक् ।
मामालिङ्ग्य निराकारं विविधाकारधारिणी ॥ ३७ ॥
मायैवैका हि नृत्यन्ती मोहयत्यखिला धियः ।
पुंसां भेदो बुद्धिभेदादम्बुभेदाद् यथा रवेः ॥ ३८ ॥
व्योम्नश्च छिद्ररूपेण भेदः कुम्भादिभेदतः ।
अतः शुद्धो बुद्धमुक्तः सर्वदा सर्वगोऽव्ययः ॥ ३९ ॥
अहमन्ये च तत्त्वाऽहो शत्रुमित्रादिधीर्मृषा ।
ब्रह्मणीशे हराविन्द्रे सर्वभूतगणे तथा ॥ ४० ॥
उत्तमाधममध्यत्वविभागो मायया मृषा ।
त्रिगुणात्मकमायायास्त्रैविध्यादात्मनोऽपि हि ॥ ४१ ॥
उत्तमाधममध्यत्वत्रैविध्यं नैव हि स्वतः ।
यथा देहे तथाऽन्यत्र चित्प्रकाशोऽयमव्ययः ॥ ४२ ॥
व्यक्तताव्यक्ततामात्रभेदो ह्यन्तरबाह्ययोः ।
एवमन्येऽपि पुरुषा बद्धमुक्ताविशेषतः ॥ ४३ ॥

ईशानीशाविशेषाच्च पुरुषार्थो न मेऽस्त्यतः।
महानिद्रैव मे साध्वी दुःखभोगहरा प्रिया ॥ ४४ ॥
अप्रिया मूढचित्तानामसाध्वी धीहतात्मनाम्।
चिदादर्शे मयि धियो यद्यपि प्रतिबिम्बनम् ॥ ४५ ॥
तत्त्वतो नैव दोषाय तथाऽपि त्याज्यमेव तत्।
स्वभावादस्य हेयत्वं स्वानुभूत्या हि सिध्यति ॥ ४६ ॥
यथा कोऽपि परस्याऽपि वैरूप्यं न दिदृक्षति।
स्वामिन्यारोप्याऽऽत्मदोषान् साध्वीयमनुतप्यते ॥ ४७ ॥
निर्दोषं स्वामिनं दृष्ट्वा निर्दोषा स्यात् पतिव्रता।
एवमस्या रूपभेदेऽप्येकरूपोऽस्मि सर्वदा ॥ ४८ ॥
भुञ्जानो वाऽप्यभुञ्जानस्तां मदर्थामनन्यगाम्।
यथैकरूपतोपाधियोगायोगदशास्वहो ॥ ४९ ॥
आदर्शस्याऽमलस्येव चिन्नभोदर्पणस्य मे।
दृश्यबद्बहिर्गता दोषाः साक्षात् तद्द्रष्टरि प्रभौ ॥ ५० ॥
न सन्ति मयि मोहाद्या भास्करे भास्यदोषवत्।
दुःखैर्बद्धा स्वमात्मानं त्यक्त्वा मद्भावमागता ॥ ५१ ॥
मुच्यते दुःखबन्धाद् धीर्न मे मोक्षो न बन्धनम्।
कूटस्थासङ्गचिद्धाम्नि धीदुःखप्रतिबिम्बनम् ॥ ५२ ॥
योऽन्यो बन्धो भोगरूपः सोऽपि चिद्दर्पणे मृषा।
जाग्रदादित्रयावस्थासाक्षी ताभिर्विवर्जितः ॥ ५३ ॥
अहं पूर्णश्चिदादित्य उदयास्तविवर्जितः।
दर्पणे मुखवद् विश्वं मयि बोधे न तात्त्विकम् ॥ ५४ ॥

विभुत्वेऽपि च बाह्यान्तः सुषुप्त्यादावदर्शनात् ।
मयि वाऽन्यत्र वा पुंसि केवलानुभवे विभौ ॥ ५५ ॥
भाति यत् तद्विवर्त्तो धीप्रतिबिम्बात्मकत्वतः ।
शुक्तौ रजतवद् विश्वमतो मयि न दोषकृत् ॥ ५६ ॥
मरीचौ तोयवत् तद्वद् व्योमादौ नगरादिवत् ।
कालत्रयेऽपि नाऽस्त्येव मयि विश्वं सनातने ॥ ५७ ॥
अन्यत्राऽस्त्वथवा माऽस्तु बुद्ध्यादौ मम तेन किम् ।
मयि सर्वं यथा व्योम्नि सर्वत्राऽहं यथा नभः ॥ ५८ ॥
न सर्वं मयि सर्वत्र नाऽहं चालेपतः खवत् ।
अत एवाऽविभागाख्याभेदेन क्षीरनीरवत् ॥ ५९ ॥
ज्ञानात्मकमिदं विश्वं गायन्ति परमर्षयः ।
जगन् मम मदर्थत्वान् मच्छरीरसुखादिवत् ॥ ६० ॥
यथा मम तथाऽन्येषां ममैवेति धियो भ्रमः ।
वस्तुतस्तु न कस्याऽपि किमपि व्यभिचारतः ॥ ६१ ॥
स्वामित्वस्याऽध्रुवत्वेन पान्थस्याऽऽवासगेहवत् ।
एकं चिन्मात्रमस्तीह शुद्धं शून्यं निरञ्जनम् ॥ ६२ ॥
सूक्ष्मात् सूक्ष्मतरं तत्र न जगन् न जगत्क्रिया ।
दृश्यते सर्वदृश्याढ्या स्वस्वबुद्धिपरम्परा ॥ ६३ ॥
चिन्मात्रमलमद्धादर्शे प्रतिबिम्बमुपागता ।
क्वचिद् व्यक्तं क्वचित् सूक्ष्मं नभः सर्वत्र तिष्ठति ॥ ६४ ॥
यथा तथा चिदाकाशं धीदेशेऽन्यत्र च स्थितम् ।
चिदाकाशमयं विश्वं यतोऽतो धीरितस्ततः ॥ ६५ ॥

भ्रमन्तौ तत्र तत्रैव भासतेऽर्के घटादिवत्।
धर्माधर्मौ जन्ममृत्यू सुखदुःखादि चाऽखिलम्॥ ६६॥
जाग्रत्यपि मृषा स्वप्न इव जन्मादिकं मम।
दृश्ययोगवियोगाभ्यां चितो जन्मविनाशधीः॥ ६७॥
अभिव्यक्त्यनभिव्यक्तिदोषाभ्यां शशिनो यथा।
मद्दासुषुप्तौ भवजन्ममृत्यु-
दुःस्वप्नधाराः क्षणभङ्गुरा धियः।
पश्याम्यहं ताभिरलिप्तरूपो
घनैरुपेतैर्विगतै रवेः किम्॥ ६८॥
इत्येवं सततं ध्यायन्नेकाग्रमनसा सुधीः।
साक्षात्करोत्यात्मतत्त्वं वागगोचररूपतः॥ ६९॥
स्वरूपं निर्मलं शान्तं मनस्त्यजति चेत् क्षणम्।
तदैव दृश्यसंस्कारशेषात् सङ्क्षुभ्यतीन्द्रियम्॥ ७०॥
उत्थितानुत्थितांस्तत्र इन्द्रियारीन् पुनः पुनः।
विवेकेनैव वज्रेण हन्यादिन्द्रो गिरीनिव॥ ७१॥

इति श्रीविज्ञानभिक्षुविरचिते साङ्ख्यसारे राजयोगप्रकार-
परिच्छेदः॥ * ॥

अथ सप्तमः परिच्छेदः ।

एवमात्मानुभविनो जीवन्मुक्तस्य लक्षणम् ।
स्पष्टं वक्ष्ये भवेद् येन ज्ञानाज्ञानपरीक्षणम् ॥ १ ॥
श्रवणान् मननाद् वाऽऽपि अन्यथाऽऽत्मज्ञताभ्रमात् ।
कुर्याद् गुरुमविद्वांसं स्याच् चाऽज्ञो ज्ञाभिमान्यपि ॥ २ ॥
नैश्वर्यानागतज्ञत्वादिकं ज्ञानस्य लक्षणम् ।
तद्वतेऽपि हि कैवल्यं योगभाष्यकृतेरितम् ॥ ३ ॥
श्रौतस्मार्तानि वाक्यानि ज्ञानिनो मोक्षभागिनः ।
लक्षकाण्येव लिख्यन्ते विश्वासातिशयाय वै ॥ ४ ॥
यत्र सर्वाणि भूतानि आत्मैवाऽभूद् विजानतः ।
तत्र को मोहः कः शोक एकत्वमनुपश्यतः ॥ ५ ॥
यः सर्वत्राऽनभिस्नेहस्तत् तत् प्राप्य शुभाशुभम् ।
नाऽभिनन्दति न द्वेष्टि तस्य प्रज्ञा प्रतिष्ठिता ॥ ६ ॥
न विस्मरति सर्वत्र यथा सततगो गतिम् ।
न विस्मरति निश्चैत्यं चिन्मात्रं प्राज्ञधीस्तथा ॥ ७ ॥
नोदेति नाऽस्तमायाति सुखे दुःखे मुखप्रभा ।
यथापूर्वस्थितिर्यस्य स जीवन्मुक्त उच्यते ॥ ८ ॥
यो जागर्त्ति सुषुप्तस्थो यस्य जाग्रन् न विद्यते ।
यस्य निर्वासनो बोधः स जीवन्मुक्त उच्यते ॥ ९ ॥
रागद्वेषभयादीनामनुरूपं चरन्नपि ।
योऽन्तर्व्योमवदत्यच्छः स जीवन्मुक्त उच्यते ॥ १० ॥
यस्य नाऽहङ्कृतो भावो बुद्धिर्यस्य न लिप्यते ।

कुर्वतोऽकुर्वतो वाऽपि स जीवन्मुक्त उच्यते ॥ ११ ॥
अपि शीतरुचावर्के अत्युष्णेऽपीन्दुमण्डले।
अप्यधःप्रसवत्यग्नौ जीवन्मुक्तो न चाऽन्यधीः ॥ १२ ॥
चिदात्मन इमा नित्यम्प्रस्फुरन्तीह शक्तयः।
इत्यस्याऽऽश्चर्यजालेषु नाऽभ्युदेति कुतूहलम् ॥ १३ ॥
परव्यसनिनी नारी व्यग्राऽपि गृहकर्मणि।
तदेवाऽऽस्वादयत्यन्तर्नरसङ्गरसायनम् ॥ १४ ॥
एवं तत्त्वे परे शुद्धे धीरो विश्रान्तिमागतः।
तदेवाऽऽस्वादयत्यन्तर्बहिर्व्यवहरन्नपि ॥ १५ ॥
यो नित्यमध्यात्ममयो नित्यमन्तर्मुखः सुखी।
गम्भीरश्च प्रसन्नश्च गिराविव महाह्रदः ॥ १६ ॥
परानन्दरसालुब्धो रमते स्वात्मनाऽऽत्मनि।
सर्वकर्मपरित्यागी नित्यहृष्टो निरामयः ॥ १७ ॥
न पुण्येन न पापेन नेतरेणाऽपि लिप्यते।
येन केन चिदाच्छन्नो येन केन चिदाशितः ॥ १८ ॥
यत्र क्वचन शायी च स सम्राडिव राजते।
वर्णधर्माश्रमाचारशास्त्रमन्त्रनयोज्झितः। १९ ॥
निर्गच्छति जगज्जालात् पञ्जरादिव केसरी।
वाचामतीतविषयो विषयाशादशोज्झितः ॥ २० ॥
कामप्युपगतः शोभां शरदीव नभस्तलम्।
निःस्तोत्रो निर्नमस्कारः पूज्यपूजाविवर्जितः ॥ २१ ॥
संयुक्तो वा वियुक्तो वा सदाचारनयक्रमैः।

एतावदेव खलु लिङ्गमलिङ्गमूर्त्तेः
संभ्रान्तसंसृतिचिरभ्रमनिर्वृतस्य।
तद्यस्य यन्मदनकोपविषादलोभ-
मोहापदामनुदिनं निपुणं तनुत्वम् ॥ २२ ॥

तुर्यविश्रान्तियुक्तस्य प्रतितीर्णस्य भवार्णवात्।
न कृतेनाऽकृतेनाऽर्थो न श्रुतिस्मृतिविभ्रमैः ॥ २३ ॥

तनुं त्यजतु वा तीर्थे श्वपचस्य गृहेऽथवा।
ज्ञानसम्प्राप्तिसमये मुक्त एवाऽमलाशयः ॥ २४ ॥

न मोक्षो नभसः पृष्ठे न पाताले न भूतले।
सर्वाशासंक्षये चेतःक्षयो मोक्ष इति श्रुतेः ॥ २५ ॥

जीवन्मुक्तपदं त्यक्त्वा स्वदेहे कालसात्कृते।
विशत्यदेहमुक्तत्वं पवनोऽस्पन्दतामिव ॥ २६ ॥

अनाप्ताखिलशैलादिप्रतिबिम्बे हि यादृशी।
स्याद् दर्पणे दर्पणता केवलात्मस्वरूपिणी ॥ २७ ॥

अहं त्वं जगदित्यादौ प्रशान्ते दृश्यसम्भ्रमे।
स्यात् तादृशी केवलता स्थिते द्रष्टर्यवीक्षणे ॥ २८ ॥

चिन्मात्रं चेत्यरहितमनन्तमजरं शिवम्।
अनादिमध्यनिलयं यदनाधि निरामयम् ॥ २९ ॥

न शून्यं नाऽपि चाऽऽकारं न दृश्यं न च दर्शनम्।
अनाख्यमनभिव्यक्तं तत् किञ्चिदवशिष्यते ॥ ३० ॥

इति श्रीविज्ञानभिक्षुविरचिते साङ्ख्यसारे जीवन्मुक्तिपरममुक्त्योः परिच्छेदः ॥ * ॥

इति साङ्ख्यसारस्योत्तरभागः। साङ्ख्यसाराख्यं प्रकरणं समाप्तम्।